Carnation's®

Good-and-Easy
COOKBOOK

BY VIRGINIA M. PIPER

A Benjamin Company/Rutledge Book

Color photographs by Glenn Embree and Walter Storck
Drawings by Frank Cannas

SBN 87502-009-7
The new supermarket edition prepared
and produced by Rutledge Books.
Published by The Supermarket Book Company.
For further information, contact
The Benjamin Company, Inc.
485 Madison Avenue
New York, N.Y. 10017

Library of Congress Catalog Card Number 70-121731
Printed in the United States of America

Carnation's®
Good-and-Easy
COOKBOOK

Contents

Budgets and barbecues

Men plan inflexible office budgets and expect the same system to be followed at home. Ask a woman about her household budget and she will frequently tell you it must be flexible as a pair of ski stretch pants.

Why? Dad takes over Saturday night as host to every family in the neighborhood. He also boasts, "There's nothing to cooking, really," while barbecuing the most expensive steak in the store. The price you pay for a one-meal cooking vacation is six penny-pinching dinners.

Put easy-does-it economy into seven dinners a week with ideas from the 8 Great Tomato Folks of Contadina and the Creative Carnation Evaporated Milk Cooks.

6

BARBECUE SAUCE
(makes 2½ cups sauce)

¼ cup butter
⅔ cup minced onion
½ cup brown sugar
¼ cup Worcestershire sauce
1 tablespoon vinegar

¼ teaspoon salt
1 tablespoon prepared mustard
¼ cup water
1⅔ cups tomato puree

Melt butter in saucepan. Add onion; sauté until tender. Add remaining ingredients. Simmer, uncovered, 15 minutes. Sauce may be used at once, or refrigerated and used later.

Penny-saving barbecues

FOR HAMBURGERS, broil burgers on one side until brown. Turn and spoon sauce over each burger. Cook to desired degree of doneness. Serve with toasted buns and hot Barbecue Sauce.

FOR FRANKFURTERS, make crosswise slits on each frankfurter. Barbecue about 2 minutes. Turn. Spoon franks with sauce. Continue cooking 4 to 5 minutes. Serve on buns with hot sauce.

FOR CHICKEN, place 3-pound chicken on spit. Baste generously with sauce. Continue basting with sauce while chicken cooks. Allow about 1 to 1½ hours for 3-pound chicken.

SATURDAY NIGHT COOKING VACATION. Use colorful paper plates, cups and napkins. Serve Keen Cones or Mile-High Banana Splits.

SUDDEN SHOWER? Serve ribs this way. Place ribs in shallow pans. Cover with foil. Bake in moderate oven (350° F.) 45 minutes to 1 hour. Remove foil; pour off liquid. Season ribs with salt and pepper. Cover with sauce. Bake, uncovered, 1 hour, basting ribs with sauce occasionally.

SIX PENNY-PINCHING DINNERS

TEMPTING TUNA. For 3 to 4 servings, combine 10½-ounce can cream of mushroom soup with small can Velvetized evaporated milk, 2 tablespoons chopped pimiento, 1 tablespoon grated onion, ½ cup grated process cheese in saucepan. Cook, stirring constantly until sauce is smooth. Add 1 cup drained, flaked tuna. Heat to serving temperature. Serve over cooked rice or noodles.

PENNY-WATCHERS' FRANKS AND MACARONI
(makes 6 to 8 servings)

½ cup chopped onion	½ teaspoon dry mustard
¼ cup chopped green pepper	2 cups *undiluted* Velvetized
3 tablespoons butter	evaporated milk
1 tablespoon flour	1 cup grated process cheese
¼ teaspoon seasoned salt	2 cups uncooked elbow
¼ teaspoon salt	macaroni
⅛ teaspoon pepper	1 pound frankfurters

Sauté onion and green pepper in melted butter until tender. Add flour, seasoned salt, salt, pepper and mustard. Blend until smooth. Gradually stir in evaporated milk. Stir over medium heat until slightly thickened. Add cheese; stir until cheese melts. Cook macaroni according to package directions. Drain and rinse. Cut franks into ½-inch pieces; combine with macaroni and cheese sauce. Blend. Pour macaroni mixture into 2-quart rectangular casserole. Bake in slow oven (325° F.) 25 to 30 minutes.

WORLDLY WAFFLES. Blend 1 cup boysenberry yogurt with 3 tablespoons confectioners sugar or 3 tablespoons honey until smooth. Spoon over hot waffles. Top off the meal with sizzling hot sausages and apple berry sauce.

WHAT MAKES THESE WAFFLES WORLDLY? Centuries-old yogurt. It is termed "matzoon" in Armenia, "lecen" in Egypt, "gioddu" in Italy and "dadhi" in India. The Contented Cow Company customers call it their fruit-basket product, because yogurt comes in many flavors, such as pineapple, spiced apple, strawberry, cherry and raspberry.

TOMATO-TOPPED MACARONI for 6. Drain 14½-ounce can sliced baby tomatoes. Save ⅔ cup liquid. Set 12 slices aside; chop remainder. Sauté ½ cup minced onion, ¾ cup thinly sliced celery and 1 crushed garlic clove in 3 tablespoons margarine 3 to 4 minutes. Stir in 3 tablespoons flour. Gradually stir in tomato liquid, 1 cup milk, chopped tomatoes, ½ teaspoon salt, ⅛ teaspoon pepper, 3 or 4 drops hot pepper sauce, 2 teaspoons dry mustard and 1½ cups shredded sharp Cheddar cheese. Cook over medium heat until cheese melts and sauce is smooth and slightly thickened. Stir in 3 cups cooked macaroni, 2 cups diced leftover ham. Pour into 12 x 7½ x 2-inch baking dish. Sprinkle with 1½ cups buttered soft bread cubes. Bake in moderate oven (350° F.) 20 minutes. Cut 3 process cheese slices in halves; place cheese and tomato slices on macaroni. Sprinkle generously with Parmesan cheese. Bake 10 minutes.

ROSY BAKED BEAN SANDWICHES
(makes 8 servings)

2 cups canned baked beans
⅔ cup tomato paste
¾ cup chopped onion
¼ cup sweet pickle relish
1 tablespoon prepared mustard

1 tablespoon brown sugar
½ teaspoon salt
8 toasted bread slices
4 partially fried bacon slices

Mix baked beans, tomato paste, onion, relish, mustard, sugar and salt. Spread to edges of each toast slice. Top with half bacon slice. Broil 4 inches from heat until bacon is crisp. Serve with mugs of hot cocoa.

CORN AND BACON BAKE. For 6 servings, combine 3½ cups cream-style corn, ¼ cup chopped green pepper and ¼ cup chopped onion. Place half of mixture in bottom of 9 x 6 x 2-inch buttered baking dish. Prepare 1½ cups coarsely crushed crackers. Place half of crackers on corn. Add remaining corn. Top with crumbs. Mix 1 cup *undiluted* Velvetized evaporated milk, ½ teaspoon salt and ⅛ teaspoon pepper. Pour over corn. Top with 2 tablespoons butter. Bake in moderate oven (350° F.). Serve with crisp bacon.

Low on calories, high on energy

CUT CALORIES with the right nibbles. For after-school, before-dinner or nightcap snacks, keep a supply of carrot cuts, celery curls or fruit handy. Cut chips and cookies off the nibble list. The pounds that never go *on* need never come *off*!

SERVE energy-packed meals. Avoid the strenuous diets that make every family member cross, jumpy and irritable. Broil rather than fry meats, chicken or seafood.

CONTINUE DESSERT, but count calories. Rather than overly rich cakes and pies, use desserts such as Calorie-Light Orange Chill.

AVOID the "no breakfast" nonsense with lower-calorie breakfast-in-a-glass. Place tall glasses and envelopes of Instant Breakfast on a tray near the refrigerator. Let each of the family select a favorite flavor.

SNEAKY NUTRITIONIST, that's you! When mixed with 8 ounces of milk, Instant Breakfast combines Vitamin C of tomatoes, egg protein, minerals found in bacon and buttered toast energy. There's a whole wide world of breakfast variety, too, with the many flavors from Carnation—chocolate, coffee, vanilla and butterscotch, to mention just a few.

11

INSTANT CALORIE-LIGHT ORANGE CHILL
(makes 6 servings)

1 cup orange juice

1 tablespoon (1 envelope) unflavored gelatine

1 cup (8¾-ounce can) fruit cocktail and syrup

½ cup chilled orange juice

½ cup Carnation Instant Nonfat Dry Milk

2 tablespoons lemon juice

¼ cup sugar

Place orange juice and gelatine in saucepan. Cook over low heat, stirring occasionally until gelatine dissolves. Add fruit cocktail and syrup. Chill until consistency of unbeaten egg whites. Pour chilled orange juice in mixing bowl. Add nonfat dry milk and whip until soft peaks form (3 to 4 minutes). Add lemon juice and continue whipping until stiff (3 to 4 minutes). Gradually add sugar. Fold gelatine mixture into whipped Instant. Spoon into a 1-quart mold. Chill until set. Unmold and garnish with whipped Instant topping and fruit sections.

SCALLOP-TOMATO BROIL
(makes 4 servings)

¼ cup oil

1 pound fresh or frozen scallops

½ cup chopped onion

½ cup chopped green pepper

1 crushed clove garlic

2 cups tomato sauce

¾ teaspoon salt

⅛ teaspoon pepper

¼ teaspoon basil

Grated Parmesan cheese

Buttered soft bread crumbs
or croutons

Heat 2 tablespoons oil in large skillet. Add scallops. Cook, turning often, 5 to 7 minutes or until scallops are tender. Remove scallops; wipe skillet clean. Sauté onion, green pepper and garlic with *remaining* 2 tablespoons oil. Add all remaining ingredients except scallops. Simmer 10 minutes; add scallops. Heat thoroughly. Spoon into 4 shells. Top with cheese. Sprinkle crumbs around edges. Broil about 5 inches from heat 3 to 5 minutes or until cheese melts and crumbs brown.

CUCUMBER TOMATO NIBBLES
(makes 20 to 24)

½ cup sour cream
¼ cup deviled ham
¼ teaspoon cayenne pepper
1 teaspoon onion salt
1 tablespoon poppy seeds

2 cups sliced, scored cucumber
1⅔ cups drained sliced baby
   tomatoes
1 cup cooked, cleaned shrimp

Blend sour cream, deviled ham, cayenne, onion salt and poppy seeds thoroughly. Spread half sour cream mixture on cucumber slices. Place tomato slice on top. Spread remaining sour cream mixture on tomato slice. Top with shrimp. Chill.

DOES SCORING A CUCUMBER sound like some new sports contest? No. It is a kitchen term for gently running fork tines down the sides of a cucumber to create scalloped edges on each thin slice.

THINK SLIM, but don't skip meals. This doesn't help your disposition, and it can damage your health. Use these Tops in Toppings for seafoods, salads and fruits!

SEAFOOD DILL SAUCE. For 1 cup sauce, combine 1 cup plain yogurt, 1 teaspoon dillweed, 1 tablespoon vinegar, ½ teaspoon sugar, 1 teaspoon salt, ¼ teaspoon seasoned pepper, 1 teaspoon Worcestershire sauce. Mix well. Chill 1 hour, then serve over broiled seafood.

ROQUEFORT TOPPING. For 1½ cups topping, blend 1 cup plain yogurt, ¼ teaspoon celery salt, ⅛ teaspoon paprika, ½ teaspoon salt, ½ teaspoon seasoned salt, ¼ cup mayonnaise. Stir until smooth. Add 3 ounces crumbled Roquefort cheese. Serve on crisp salad greens.

TOUCH-OF-MINT FRUIT TOPPING. For 1 cup, combine 1 cup pineapple yogurt, ¼ cup confectioners sugar, ⅛ teaspoon mint extract, 1 drop green food color. Blend. Serve chilled over fruit.

Do-ahead dining

The fascination of food can't be appreciated when it must be inhaled at the office, munched on a class-to-class run or nibbled between laundry loads. Neither should lovely wedding gifts of silver, crystal and china remain tucked away in unreachable closets and drawers.

Do-Ahead Dining adds a special touch to simple foods and gives the hostess an opportunity to enjoy her own party. No need to compete with the cooking talents of a French chef or plan a meal that would take the talents of a five-man catering staff, if yours is a do-it-yourself household. THINK! Concentrate on one spectacular, and dress up dinner with colorful mats, crystal, silver and china hidden too long.

HOSTESS a Sunday brunch for friends when older children can baby-sit the little ones. Baked Deviled Eggs with Ham does take some beforehand preparation time, but refrigerate the dish overnight and pop it in the oven for brunch.

AVOID too many last-minute details. A No-Salad-Tonight Vegetable Dip tray in the living room eliminates one mealtime task.

SAVE the budget with seasoning secrets to perk up less expensive main dishes. When it is plentiful, serve Roast Pork with a Polynesian Touch or try Bombay Chicken.

END some confusion at a sit-down dinner. When you serve Company's-Coming Shrimp Chafing Dish and rice, each guest can help himself at the buffet. Place Shortcut Antipasto on the table and everyone sits down at once!

GLAMORIZE the ever-popular molded salad with a Skyscraper Tropicana Salad prepared in a tall mold and served on a pedestal cake dish. (If the mold seems too small for your treasured dish, garnish the edges with mandarin oranges and grapes.)

14

COMPANY'S-COMING SHRIMP CHAFING DISH
(makes 8 to 10 servings)

½ cup chopped green pepper
1 cup chopped onion
¼ cup butter
¼ cup flour
3⅓ cups *undiluted* Velvetized evaporated milk
2 tablespoons tomato paste
1 teaspoon salt
¼ teaspoon pepper
¼ teaspoon mace

¼ teaspoon ginger
1 teaspoon Worcestershire sauce
1 tablespoon lemon juice
2 7½-ounce cans crab meat
2 12-ounce packages cooked, drained, rinsed frozen shrimp
½ cup drained whole mushrooms

Sauté green pepper and onion in butter. Blend in flour. Gradually stir in evaporated milk. Cook over low heat, stirring constantly until thickened. Add tomato paste. Mix well. Add remaining ingredients. Cook, stirring constantly, 10 minutes or until thoroughly heated. Serve in chafing dish. Top with parsley. Serve with cooked rice.

BAKED DEVILED EGGS WITH HAM
(makes 8 to 10 servings)

10 hard-cooked eggs
¼ cup minced parsley
1 tablespoon prepared mustard
¼ cup mayonnaise
2 teaspoons vinegar
½ teaspoon seasoned salt
10 square slices boiled ham

2 tablespoons finely chopped onion
1 tablespoon chopped pimiento
⅛ teaspoon dillweed
10½-ounce can cream of mushroom soup
⅔ cup *undiluted* Velvetized evaporated milk

Halve eggs and remove yolks. Mash yolks. Combine with 2 tablespoons minced parsley, mustard, mayonnaise, vinegar and seasoned salt. Mix well. Fill whites with yolk mixture. Put two halves together. Place each egg diagonally on ham slice. Fold ham around egg. Secure with toothpicks. Place eggs in 12 x 7½ x 2-inch baking dish. Mix remaining ingredients and remaining parsley. Pour over eggs. Bake in moderate oven (350° F.) 20 to 25 minutes. Garnish with additional parsley.

SKYSCRAPER TROPICANA SALAD
(makes 10 to 12 servings)

11-ounce can mandarin oranges
13½-ounce can pineapple
 chunks
1 cup water
2 3-ounce packages lemon-
 flavored gelatin
2 cups cottage cheese

1 cup halved, seeded Tokay
 grapes or drained, canned
 seedless grapes
1 cup coarsely chopped apple
½ cup finely crushed
 gingersnaps

Drain mandarin oranges and pineapple chunks, reserving liquids. Combine liquids to make *1 cup*. Add water. Bring just to a boil. Pour over gelatin. Stir to dissolve. Chill to consistency of unbeaten egg white. Stir in mandarin oranges, pineapple chunks, cottage cheese, grapes and apple. Pour into 6½-cup mold. Sprinkle crushed gingersnaps over gelatin. Press lightly with fingertips. Chill until firm.

ROAST PORK WITH A POLYNESIAN TOUCH. For 6 servings, mix 2/3 cup tomato paste, ¼ cup soy sauce and 2 tablespoons brown sugar in small saucepan. Drain 8½-ounce can pineapple; save juice. Add drained pineapple and ¼ *cup pineapple juice* to tomato mixture. Heat just to boiling, stirring constantly. Trim excess fat from meat. Place 3 to 3½-pound pork loin roast on rack in shallow pan. Sprinkle generously with seasoned salt. Brush ⅓ *cup sauce* over meat. Cover meat loosely with foil. Bake in slow oven (325° F.) 2 hours. Remove foil. Bake additional 30 minutes. Add remaining pineapple juice to remaining sauce. Heat to serving temperature. Serve with roast.

COOKING HINT. Perhaps you've never thought of using tomato paste for anything but spaghetti sauce or Italian dishes. The Contadina Kitchens use it for marinades, stews or even shortcut Stroganoff. Adds a new flavor touch to meats.

NO-SALAD-TONIGHT VEGETABLE DIP. For 1½ cups dip, beat 1 cup cottage cheese until smooth. Add ½ cup sour cream, 1 teaspoon dillweed, 1 teaspoon grated onion, ½ teaspoon salt, ⅛ teaspoon pepper, ¼ teaspoon paprika and blend thoroughly. Chill 1 to 2 hours to blend flavors. Serve dip on a tray, surrounded with cold celery and carrot sticks, green pepper strips and radishes, cauliflower cuts and ripe pitted olives.

WHEN THERE'S NO "DO AHEAD" time to whip up and chill dips, use shortcuts. There are usually a supply of ready to use dips in the refrigerated foods section of your market. Take advantage of them!

LATE-ARRIVING GUESTS may have been house-hunting—for *your* house. Use reflector tape to put your name on the mailbox.

BOMBAY CHICKEN
(makes 6 servings)

¼ cup flour	2 tablespoons chopped parsley
1 teaspoon salt	1 tablespoon butter
⅛ teaspoon pepper	1½ teaspoons curry powder
3 to 3½ pounds chicken pieces	2 cups tomato sauce
¼ cup butter	½ teaspoon salt
1 crushed clove garlic	½ cup raisins
⅓ cup minced onion	

Combine flour, salt and pepper in paper bag. Coat chicken with flour mixture. Melt ¼ cup butter in 13-x 9-x 2-inch baking dish. Arrange chicken in dish, skin side up. Bake in very hot oven (450° F.) 30 minutes. Sauté garlic, onion and parsley in 1 tablespoon butter in saucepan. Stir in curry powder. Add remaining ingredients. Simmer rapidly, uncovered, 10 to 15 minutes. Remove chicken from oven. Reduce oven to 350° F. Spoon sauce over chicken. Bake additional 30 to 40 minutes or until chicken is tender.

SHORTCUT ANTIPASTO. Drain 1⅔ cups Italian Style tomatoes. Cut tomatoes in half lengthwise. Drain well on paper towels. Blend tomatoes with 1 6-ounce jar marinated artichoke hearts. Season lightly with salt and pepper. Chill 2 hours and serve on crisp lettuce instead of the usual green salad.

Hints for the host

When the last guest dusts out the door, don't sprint for your slippers. Help tidy up. It was *your* party, too.

CLEAR up cooking odors and cigarette smoke in minutes by burning a candle in each room.

BANK the fire and secure the fireplace screen so no coals will pop out on the carpeting or draperies during the night.

EMPTY ashtrays into a metal container and be sure there's nothing left to smolder in the upholstery of a favorite easy chair.

CARRY the overflowing wastebasket out now. Good intentions are easily forgotten in the morning rush.

Easy entertaining

CHEESE SPAGHETTI FOR 12
(makes 12 servings)

1½ pounds ground chuck
3 cups tomato sauce
4½ cups water
3 packages spaghetti sauce mix
¾ teaspoon salt
1½ pounds spaghetti
¼ cup butter
⅓ cup flour

1½ teaspoons salt
2 cups Velvetized
    evaporated milk
1 cup water
2 cups shredded process
    American cheese
⅓ cup grated Parmesan cheese

Brown chuck in large saucepan. Pour off fat. Add tomato sauce, the 4½ cups water, spaghetti sauce mix and the ¾ teaspoon salt. Simmer, uncovered, stirring often for 30 minutes. Break spaghetti into thirds. Cook according to package directions. Rinse spaghetti. Drain and keep warm. Melt butter in saucepan. Stir in flour and the 1½ teaspoons salt. Add evaporated milk and water slowly, stirring over medium heat until thickened. Add 1½ cups American cheese and the Parmesan cheese. Stir until melted. To prepare 2 13 x 9 x 2-inch casseroles, divide spaghetti, tomato sauce and cheese sauce in half. In each casserole, layer ingredients as follows: spaghetti, half of tomato sauce, cheese sauce, spaghetti and remaining tomato sauce. Top with ¼ cup of the American cheese. Bake in moderate oven (350° F.) 15 to 25 minutes or until bubbly. Serve at once.

EASY ENTERTAINING HINT! Spaghetti may be prepared in advance and refrigerated. Add shredded American cheese just before baking. Bake as above for 20 to 30 minutes or until bubbly. Add ½ cup chopped pitted ripe olives if you are having *extra special* guests.

TOMATO-STEAK SUPPER IN A SKILLET
(makes 4 to 6 servings)

2 pounds ½-inch-thick
  sirloin tip steak
Seasoned salt
Seasoned pepper
2 cups thinly sliced onion rings

½ teaspoon garlic puree
¼ cup melted butter
1⅔ cups drained sliced
  baby tomatoes
Dried shredded parsley

Cut meat into serving pieces. Sprinkle generously with seasoned salt and pepper. Pound seasonings into meat, but do not pound thin. Sauté onion and garlic in butter 2 to 3 minutes. Add meat; brown on both sides over medium heat, 5 to 10 minutes. Keep onions on top of meat as it cooks. When meat is browned, arrange tomatoes on top of steaks. Sprinkle with parsley. Cover. Heat 5 minutes over low heat. Place on warm serving plate and serve immediately.

AFTER-THE-GAME CHICKEN AND RICE
(makes 6 servings)

2 6-ounce packages chicken-
  flavored rice
⅓ cup flour
1 teaspoon seasoned salt
½ teaspoon poultry seasoning
2½ to 3 pounds frying
  chicken pieces

3 tablespoons melted butter
1 cup sour cream
1¼ cups canned cream of
  chicken soup
2 cups sliced fresh mushrooms
Paprika

Prepare rice as label directs. Combine flour, seasoned salt and poultry seasoning. Coat chicken. Place skin side up in 13 x 9 x 3-inch baking dish. Cover with butter. Bake, uncovered, in hot oven (425° F.) 45 minutes. Reduce heat to 350° F. Place rice in casserole. Top with chicken. Mix sour cream, soup and mushrooms; pour over chicken. Sprinkle with paprika. Cover. Bake at 350° F. 20 to 25 minutes.

AFTER-THE-SWIM FRUIT PIZZA FOR TEEN-AGERS
(makes 8 to 10 servings)

2 cups biscuit mix	¼ cup shredded coconut
3 tablespoons sugar	¼ cup firmly packed brown
½ cup homogenized milk	sugar
¼ cup melted butter	1 tablespoon flour
2 cups cottage cheese	1 teaspoon cinnamon
2½ cups well-drained	1 tablespoon melted butter
fruit cocktail	¼ cup chopped nuts

Combine biscuit mix, sugar, milk and ¼ cup butter. Stir with fork until dough leaves sides of bowl. Turn onto lightly floured board. Knead until smooth. Flour hands well. Press dough into 13-inch pizza pan, making edges of dough slightly higher than center. Bake in hot oven (425° F.) 10 minutes or until golden brown. Cool on wire rack 5 to 10 minutes. Spread cottage cheese over crust. Place fruit cocktail on cottage cheese. Top with coconut. Combine brown sugar, flour, cinnamon, 1 tablespoon butter and nuts. Mix well. Sprinkle mixture over fruit cocktail and coconut. Broil 4 to 6 inches from heat 1 to 3 minutes or until brown sugar mixture is slightly melted. Serve immediately.

SHORTCUT SPAGHETTI SAUCE
(makes about 5 cups)

½ cup chopped onion	2 cups water
½ cup chopped green pepper	1 package spaghetti sauce mix
2½ ounces sliced pepperoni	1 cup grated Romano cheese
2 tablespoons oil	¼ cup cracker meal
⅔ cup tomato paste	1 egg
1⅔ cups Italian Style tomatoes	

Sauté onion, green pepper and pepperoni in oil in saucepan. Add tomato paste, tomatoes, water and spaghetti sauce mix. Stir to break tomatoes. Simmer, uncovered, 20 minutes. Stir occasionally. Combine Romano cheese, cracker meal and egg. Mix thoroughly. Shape into 14 to 16 small balls. Add to sauce. Simmer additional 10 to 15 minutes. Serve over spaghetti.

CONFETTI SOLE BAKE
(makes 6 to 8 servings)

2 pounds fillet of sole
1 teaspoon salt
⅛ teaspoon white pepper
1 tablespoon parsley flakes
½ cup finely chopped onion

½ cup chopped green pepper
1 tablespoon diced green chiles
1⅔ cups well-drained
   sliced baby tomatoes
¼ cup melted butter

Place half of fish in bottom of buttered 12 x 7¾ x 2-inch baking dish. Sprinkle with half of salt, pepper and parsley. Top with onion, green pepper, green chiles and all but six of the tomato slices. Brush with half of butter. Top with remaining fish. Brush fish with remaining butter. Sprinkle with remaining salt, pepper and parsley. Garnish with six tomato slices. Bake in hot oven (400° F.) 20 to 30 minutes or until fish is flaky.

SUMMER SUPPER ON A PLATTER. For 6 guests, drain 14½-ounce can sliced baby tomatoes. Drain slices thoroughly on paper towels. Chill. Combine 2 cups cottage cheese, ¼ cup sliced green onion, ¼ cup sliced ripe olives, ⅓ cup chopped celery, 1 teaspoon seasoned salt, ¼ teaspoon pepper and ¼ teaspoon crushed dillweed. Mix well; chill. At serving time, place cottage cheese mixture, ripe avocado slices, sliced baby tomatoes on lettuce-lined platter. Serve hot rolls and iced tea, and let each guest help himself.

AHUACATL! That's a tongue-twister from South America. The name is so difficult to pronounce that we call this delicious food avocado. It was first used by the pre-Incan races of Peru, Yucatán and Mexico. How can we be sure? Look closely at their pottery and sculpture. You'll find avocados there.

23

ONION ROLL CHEESEWICHES. For 8 servings, slice 4 onion rolls in half. Spread with 3 tablespoons softened butter. Sprinkle with 1½ teaspoons garlic powder and 1 tablespoon partially crushed oregano leaves. Place under broiler 5 inches from heat for 1 to 2 minutes or until lightly toasted. Sprinkle rolls with ¼ cup minced onion, ¼ cup sliced stuffed olives and ½ cup drained sliced mushrooms. Cover with 8 squares of process American cheese. Top with tomato slices. Broil 2 to 3 minutes longer or until cheese is slightly melted. Serve immediately with cold glasses of milk. Use sherbet and cookies for dessert.

GRANDMOTHER'S COFFEE-TIME TREAT
(makes 9-inch cake)

1 cup margarine	1 teaspoon vanilla
1¼ cups sugar	½ cup chopped mixed nuts
2 eggs	1 teaspoon cinnamon
1 cup strawberry yogurt	2 tablespoons sugar
2 cups sifted flour	1 10-ounce package thawed,
½ teaspoon soda	frozen sliced strawberries
1½ teaspoons baking powder	

Combine margarine, sugar and eggs in large bowl. Beat until light and fluffy. Add yogurt. Beat until smooth. Sift flour, soda and baking powder together. Add to creamed mixture; blend well. Stir in vanilla. Spoon *half* of batter into well-buttered and floured 9-inch tube pan. Mix nuts, cinnamon and sugar; spoon over batter. Spoon remaining batter over cinnamon mixture. Bake in moderate oven (350° F.) 50 to 60 minutes or until toothpick comes out clean. Cool on wire rack until lukewarm. Turn out onto platter. Top with berries.

GET EVERYTHING TO THE TABLE ON TIME
... with an Easy Entertaining *backwards* timetable! Make a menu, time each part, then tape it near range or refrigerator. Before calling guests to dinner, make a quick check. Who wants to miss the special salad that was overlooked in the last-minute rush?

Main dish know-how

BUY WISELY. Look for the meat inspection stamp as an assurance that the meat has come from healthy animals and has been closely supervised during preparation for market. *Learn* the differences in grades of inspected meats. The six grades (Prime, Choice, Good, Standard, Commercial and Utility) are based on the general contour of the carcass; the quality, amount and distribution of fat; the firmness and strength of meat tissue and fibers. Prices vary according to grade.

COOK PROPERLY. Every grade and cut of meat can be made tender and palatable. Meat packers or associations will gladly send you free material on selection, buying and preparation of various meat cuts. When roasting meats, beef may be cooked rare, medium or well done, according to your family's taste. Veal and pork should be cooked well done and lamb is cooked medium or well done.

STORE CAREFULLY. For meats you'll be using within several days, store loosely wrapped in wax paper or as your refrigerator manual directs. For freezer storage, wrap family-sized servings in moistureproof and vaporproof wrapping (such as freezer weight foil or freezer wrapping paper). Freeze quickly at below-zero temperatures and store at 0° F. Date and label all frozen meats, and use "first in, first out" cooking system.

Any tender cut of beef, veal, pork or lamb may be roasted. It's so easy to prepare a roast (and have leftovers for other weekday meals) this way. . . .

1. PLACE meat, fat side up, on rack in shallow roasting pan. Season with salt and pepper.
2. INSERT meat thermometer into roast so that the bulb is in the center of the largest muscle. If you don't have a meat thermometer, consult your range manual or meat booklet for roasting time and temperature. Time will vary with the size of your roast.
3. DON'T add water. Leave the roast uncovered.
4. ROAST in slow oven (300° F. to 350° F.) to the desired degree of doneness. Place roast on warm serving plate and cover while making gravy.

NO-MYSTERY GRAVY

Use equal amounts of slightly cooled meat drippings and flour for each cup of liquid added. Tastes vary on gravy consistency, so take your pick. But remember: gravy thickens on standing.

	DRIPPINGS	FLOUR	LIQUID
For thinner gravy	*1 tablespoon*	*1 tablespoon*	*1 cup*
For medium gravy	*2 tablespoons*	*2 tablespoons*	*1 cup*

Measuring isn't enough. For never-a-lump gravy, blend *cooled* drippings and flour in heavy saucepan or skillet over *low* heat. Gradually add liquid, stirring constantly until gravy is thickened and smooth. Season to taste.

GOOD-AND-EASY GRAVY HINT. For liquid, use water, water with a bouillon cube added, or for extra flavor, vegetable or sliced baby tomato liquid to prepare beef or lamb gravy. For chicken, turkey, pork or ham, use homogenized milk or Velvetized evaporated milk mixed with an equal amount of water.

No need to suffer "good gravy nerves" when your in-laws or the boss and his wife are coming to dinner. There are other ways to solve the problem. Tangy Tomato Relish adds a Far Eastern flavor touch to broiled meats. Baked Chicken That Makes Its Own Gravy lets you enjoy guests.

TANGY TOMATO RELISH. For 1¼ cups sauce, combine in a saucepan 1⅔ cups Italian Style tomatoes, ¼ cup canned whole cranberry sauce, 2 tablespoons raisins, 1 tablespoon sugar, ½ teaspoon ginger, ½ teaspoon salt and ⅛ teaspoon cayenne. Break up tomatoes. Simmer, stirring often, 30 minutes. Serve chilled or at room temperature with meats.

BAKED CHICKEN THAT MAKES ITS OWN GRAVY
(makes 6 servings)

3 to 3½ pounds frying chicken pieces
¼ cup flour
¼ cup melted butter
2 cups drained whole canned onions
¼ pound sliced mushrooms
⅔ cup *undiluted* Velvetized evaporated milk

10½-ounce can cream of mushroom soup
1 cup grated process American cheese
½ teaspoon salt
⅛ teaspoon pepper
Dash of paprika

Coat chicken with flour. Arrange in single layer with skins down in melted butter in 13 x 9 x 2-inch baking dish. Bake, uncovered, in moderately hot oven (425° F.) 30 minutes. Turn chicken. Bake until brown, 15 to 20 minutes longer or until tender. Remove baking dish from oven; reduce temperature to 325° F. Pour off excess fat. Add onions and mushrooms to chicken. Combine evaporated milk, soup, cheese, salt and pepper. Pour over chicken. Sprinkle with paprika. Cover with foil. Return to oven and continue baking 15 to 20 minutes.

> GOLDEN PEPPER? Well, it was *almost* worth its weight in gold in the days of the first Queen Elizabeth. To prevent thievery, workers who unloaded pepper cargoes were dressed in "theftproof" suits without pockets. Even today, black pepper is still king of the spices. We consume over 350,000,000 pounds each year.

Holiday hints

Holidays are family-gathering times, and you wouldn't have it any other way. Such get-togethers are fun for everyone—including you, provided you do some careful advance planning, and if you're not too proud to accept the help that you're bound to need.

SHARING Thanksgiving, Christmas, Easter and other occasions with friends and relatives can be pleasure all the way if you let "sharing" mean that everyone pitches in. All the out-of-town guests don't have to be lodged in one place. Perhaps other relatives in your own town can put some of them up. Or some can—and may, indeed, prefer to—stay at a hotel or motel. Check neighbors' holiday plans, too. Some of them may be going away, in which case there may be bedrooms available right in the neighborhood in exchange for "house sitting." Don't feel conscience-stricken because you're not entertaining all the guests in your own home. Peace and privacy for a part of their stay will be as welcome to them as it will be to you.

SHY about making suggestions when someone asks "What can I bring?" Don't be! In addition to all the joy of reunions, they do mean a lot of hard work, and they can be death on the food budget as well. So accept such offers in the spirit in which they're made, and be thankful that you have such a good-hearted, generous family.

USE a combination of do-aheads, traditional holiday foods and leftovers in disguise. Make cake layers for a Christmas Wreath Cake or Spring Daffodil Cake, Freeze-It-and-Forget-It Fruit Salad for the freezer. Give traditional Christmas dinner foods a new look as Turkey Salad Ring or Turkey in a Stuffing Crust.

AVOID crises. Organize the favorite family recipes for each holiday and purchase ingredients ahead of time. Sounds preachy? Every holiday season, the Carnation Food Service Center is besieged with frantic requests for those Traditional Carnation Pumpkin Pie and Five-Minute Fudge

Velvetized evaporated milk favorites. You may not believe this, but some phone calls come *collect*!

FRUIT SALAD DRESSING. For 1 cup dressing, combine a 3-ounce package softened cream cheese with ⅓ cup *undiluted* Velvetized evaporated milk. Beat until smooth. Add ⅓ cup more Velvetized evaporated milk, beating until blended. Add 2 tablespoons lime juice, 1 teaspoon crushed mint flakes, 1 teaspoon chives, ⅛ teaspoon crushed tarragon leaves, ⅛ teaspoon salt, 1 tablespoon sugar and ¼ teaspoon celery seed. Stir vigorously until blended. Chill. Stir well and serve on grapefruit and orange sections garnished with fresh berries.

CHICKEN CRAB MEAT CHAFING DISH
(makes 6 to 8 servings)

10½ -ounce can cream of mushroom soup
10½ -ounce can cream of chicken soup
1 cup *undiluted* Velvetized evaporated milk
1 tablespoon grated onion

⅛ teaspoon paprika
1 cup diced cooked chicken
1¼ cups flaked cooked crab meat
½ cup drained sliced mushrooms

Blend soups, Velvetized evaporated milk, onion and paprika in saucepan. Heat to just below boiling over medium heat, stirring constantly. Add remaining ingredients. Heat to serving temperature. Place in chafing dish, garnished with pimiento and parsley, and serve in patty shells.

Hints for the holiday hostess

THOUGHTFUL GUESTS aren't mind readers. Though many guests would like to do some step-saving jobs, they're hesitant to scurry around your kitchen or use your household appliances. Cultivate cooperation by writing or typing instructions for use of the dishwasher, washer and dryer. Tape the "M.O." to the appropriate appliance.

TRAY UP breakfast china, glasses and silver the night before. Also write out the breakfast menu and set up the coffee pot. First one up "perks" the coffee and begins breakfast for the crowd.

COCKTAIL KABOBS. Place 1 pineapple chunk, 1 cocktail wiener and 1 cocktail onion on each toothpick. Place on broiler pan 4 inches from heat. Broil 2 to 3 minutes on each side or until heated. Heat 15-ounce can Italian Cookbook Sauce to serving temperature. Serve with Kabobs.

DEVILED EGGS. Cut 6 hard-cooked eggs in half lengthwise. Remove yolks; mash in bowl. Add 3 tablespoons mayonnaise, 1 teaspoon prepared mustard, ½ teaspoon vinegar, ½ teaspoon Worcestershire sauce. Mix until creamy. Spoon egg-yolk mixture back into egg whites. Sprinkle with paprika or finely chopped parsley.

TANGY HAM DIP. Mix 1 cup sour cream, 2 3-ounce cans deviled ham, 2 teaspoons chopped chives, 1 tablespoon prepared horseradish and ¼ teaspoon Worcestershire sauce in bowl. Blend well. Chill 1 hour; serve with potato or corn chips.

FREEZE-IT-AND-FORGET-IT FRUIT SALAD
(makes about 12 servings)

¾ cup syrup drained from canned fruit
1 slightly beaten egg
¼ cup sugar
½ teaspoon salt
1½ tablespoons flour
2 tablespoons vinegar
1 cup drained diced canned pears

¾ cup drained pineapple tidbits
3 mashed medium ripe bananas
½ cup chopped maraschino cherries
⅔ cup *undiluted* Velvetized evaporated milk
1 tablespoon lemon juice

Combine syrup, egg, sugar, salt, flour and vinegar in saucepan. Cook over medium heat, stirring constantly until thickened. Cool. Add fruits to cooled sauce. Chill evaporated milk in refrigerator tray until soft ice crystals form around edges of tray (10 to 15 minutes). Whip until stiff (1 minute). Add lemon juice; whip very stiff (1 minute). Fold into fruit mixture. Spoon into 6-cup mold. Freeze until firm (about 5 to 6 hours).

THE TRADITIONAL CARNATION PUMPKIN PIE
(makes one 9-inch pie)

2 slightly beaten eggs
1½ cups canned pumpkin
1 cup sugar
½ teaspoon salt
1 teaspoon cinnamon
¼ teaspoon ginger

¼ teaspoon cloves
¼ teaspoon nutmeg
1⅔ cups *undiluted* Carnation evaporated milk
9-inch single crust unbaked pie shell

Combine eggs, pumpkin, sugar, salt and spices. Gradually add Carnation. Mix well. Pour into unbaked pie shell. Bake in hot oven (425° F.) 15 minutes; reduce to moderate heat (350° F.) and continue baking about 40 minutes or until knife inserted near center of pie comes out clean. Cool before serving.

WONDER WHY this pie has become traditional? It was perfected with Carnation Evaporated Milk . . . the Velvetized cooking milk for smooth pumpkin pie, custards, sauces and icings, too.

34

SNOWMAN CUPCAKES. Mix and bake cupcakes as package mix directs. Fasten 2 cooled cupcakes together bottom-to-bottom with toothpicks. Frost with Buttery Smooth Icing, page 37. Fasten marshmallow on top for head. Use 2 cloves for eyes, cinnamon candies for mouth and coat buttons. Top with candied green pineapple slice for "hat."

TURKEY SALAD RING
(makes about 12 servings)

1½ cups cooked cubed turkey
½ cup chopped celery
⅓ cup sliced ripe olives
2 tablespoons grated onion
2 tablespoons minced parsley
1 cup mayonnaise
2 teaspoons Worcestershire sauce
2 teaspoons horseradish
½ teaspoon seasoned salt
2 teaspoons prepared mustard
2 envelopes unflavored gelatine
½ cup cold water
⅔ cup *undiluted* Velvetized evaporated milk
2 tablespoons lemon juice
Cranberry sauce

Combine turkey, celery, olives, onion and parsley. Mix mayonnaise, Worcestershire, horseradish, salt and mustard. Soften gelatine in cold water. Heat over hot water to dissolve. Stir mayonnaise into dissolved gelatine. Combine gelatine and turkey mixture. Chill until mixture mounds from spoon. Chill evaporated milk in refrigerator tray until soft ice crystals form around edges of tray (10 to 15 minutes). Whip until stiff (about 1 minute). Add lemon juice. Whip very stiff (1 minute longer). Fold whipped evaporated milk into turkey. Pour into 6½-cup ring mold. Chill until firm, 2 to 3 hours. Unmold on platter. Fill center with cranberry sauce.

OLD-FASHIONED MINCEMEAT PIE. For 2-crust 8-inch pie, mix 1 cup mincemeat, 1¼ cups diced peeled apples, ½ cup seedless raisins, 1 tablespoon lemon juice in bowl. Blend 2 tablespoons cornstarch, 2 tablespoons sugar, ½ teaspoon cinnamon, ¼ teaspoon salt and ⅛ teaspoon ground cardamom. Coat fruit mixture. Add ⅔ cup *undiluted* Velvetized evaporated milk to fruits and seasonings; blend well. Place in unbaked 8-inch pie shell. Top with crust and seal edges. Make small steam vents in top crust. Bake in hot oven (400° F.) 40 minutes.

TURKEY IN A STUFFING CRUST
(makes 6 to 8 servings)

6 cups stuffing mix
1½ to 2 cups water
½ cup chopped onion
½ cup chopped celery
3 tablespoons butter
3 tablespoons flour
2½ cups *undiluted* Velvetized
  evaporated milk

½ cup sliced stuffed
  green olives
3 cups cubed cooked turkey
¼ teaspoon pepper
¼ teaspoon thyme
⅛ teaspoon poultry seasoning

Combine stuffing mix with water, using only enough liquid to moisten. Mix well. Press into buttered 12 x 7½ x 2-inch baking dish. Bake in hot oven (400° F.) 10 minutes. Sauté onion and celery in butter; add flour. Blend well, then gradually stir in evaporated milk. Stir over low heat until sauce thickens. Add remaining ingredients; blend. Place in stuffing crust. Bake in moderate oven (350° F.) 25 to 30 minutes.

FIVE-MINUTE FUDGE
(makes about 2 pounds)

2 tablespoons butter
⅔ cup *undiluted* Velvetized
  evaporated milk
1⅔ cups sugar
½ teaspoon salt

2 cups miniature marshmallows
1½ cups semisweet
  chocolate pieces
1 teaspoon vanilla
½ cup chopped nuts

Combine butter, evaporated milk, sugar and salt in saucepan over medium heat. Bring to boil. Cook 4 to 5 minutes, stirring constantly. Remove from heat. Stir in remaining ingredients. Stir vigorously 1 minute until marshmallows melt and blend. Pour into 8-inch-square buttered pan. Cool. Cut in squares.

GOOD-AND-EASY COOKING HINT. Start timing mixture when it begins to bubble around the edges of pan. Top Five-Minute Fudge with chopped nuts, crushed peppermint or toasted coconut for gifts. It's delicious!

AFTER-THE-EGG-HUNT SANDWICHES. For 6 sandwiches, mix 4 chopped hard-cooked eggs with 1 tablespoon minced ripe olives, 1 tablespoon chopped green pepper and 1 tablespoon chopped celery. Add ½ teaspoon salt, dash of pepper and ¼ cup mayonnaise. Spread on 6 buttered bread slices. Top each with second bread slice. Serve with carrot stick garnished with ripe olive.

BUTTERY SMOOTH ICING
(makes icing for two 8-inch cake layers)

¼ cup butter
3 cups sifted confectioners
  sugar

¼ cup *undiluted* Velvetized
  evaporated milk
1 teaspoon vanilla

Blend butter and sugar. Add undiluted evaporated milk and vanilla. Beat until smooth. Spread between, on sides and top of *cooled* cake layers.

CHRISTMAS WREATH CAKE. Bake favorite cake mix in two layers according to package directions. Frost with Buttery Smooth Icing. Make wreath decoration around top of cake with green candy mint leaves and red maraschino cherries.

SPRING DAFFODIL CAKE. Bake yellow cake layers according to package directions. Prepare Buttery Smooth Icing, using 2 tablespoons lemon juice and 1 teaspoon grated lemon rind in place of vanilla. Ice cake, top with daffodils made from lemon gumdrops. Use green gumdrops for stems and petals.

OFF-THE-SHELF QUICK DIP
(makes 2 cups)

1 cup salad dressing
⅓ cup *undiluted* Velvetized
  evaporated milk
1 tablespoon lemon juice
2 teaspoons chili sauce

1 tablespoon chopped chives
1 teaspoon vinegar
⅓ cup minced onion
½ cup deviled ham
1 teaspoon onion salt

Blend all ingredients well. Serve with raw vegetables, chips or a selection of crackers.

No-nonsense nutrition

There's no need to be a combination doctor, dentist and food technician to be a nutrition expert; wise food authorities have simplified food choices by using the Basic Four food groups as the simpler way to better eating habits:

MEATS, FISH AND POULTRY. These foods yield high-quality protein necessary for daily body growth, and take care of daily body wear and tear. Each day, meals should include two or more servings of beef, pork, lamb, fish, eggs or poultry. Dried beans, peas or peanut butter may be used as an alternate to meat, fish or eggs.

FRUITS AND VEGETABLES. These foods are excellent sources of minerals and vitamins. Smooth skin, the bright-eyed look, and body resistance to small infections start with enough fruits and vegetables. Include such important ones as citrus fruits or tomatoes, a dark green or yellow vegetable in the four servings of these foods every day.

BREADS AND CEREALS. Spaghetti, noodles, enriched whole-grain breads, hot or ready-prepared cold cereals provide important food elements—iron, carbohydrates for quick energy, and the valuable Vitamin B complex. The bread and cereal foods are the basis for that important morning starter, breakfast. That's the "fuel up" time for a busy day.

MILK AND DAIRY PRODUCTS. Fresh milk, evaporated milk, instant nonfat dry milk, cheese and ice cream are important, too. The *daily* calcium needs of everyone in the family can be supplied only by these products. Mother and Dad need at least one pint a day, as a beverage or in foods made with dairy products. Three to four glasses are the children's daily supply.

CHILI STEAK DINNER
(makes about 4 servings)

1½ pounds cube steaks (about 4 steaks)
Flour
2 tablespoons butter
1 tablespoon oil

15-ounce can Swiss Steak Cookbook Sauce
1 teaspoon chili powder
2 cups drained chili beans
1 cup shredded Jack cheese

Dredge steaks in flour. Brown steaks in butter and oil in large skillet. Drain off fat. Combine Swiss Steak Sauce, chili powder and beans. Pour over steaks. Simmer, uncovered, 15 minutes. Top with cheese and serve.

ITALIAN CHICKEN
(makes 6 servings)

3 to 3½ pounds frying chicken pieces
¼ cup flour
1 teaspoon salt
¼ teaspoon chili powder

⅛ teaspoon pepper
¼ cup butter
1 15-ounce can Italian Cookbook Sauce
2 cups diced zucchini

Shake chicken pieces in bag containing flour, salt, chili powder and pepper. Melt butter in frying pan. Add chicken. Cook until golden brown on both sides. Drain fat. Combine Italian Sauce and zucchini. Spoon over chicken. Cover; simmer slowly until chicken is tender (about 50 minutes). Serve with hot cooked rice, relishes and heated rolls.

PORK CHOPS, SWISS STYLE. For 4 servings, trim and score fat on 4 pork chops (½ to ¾-inch thickness). Dip chops in 1 well-beaten egg. Coat with ⅓ cup fine dry bread crumbs. Heat 3 tablespoons butter and 1 tablespoon olive oil in skillet. Brown chops thoroughly on both sides. Pour off excess fat. Add 1⅔ cups (15-ounce can) Swiss Steak Cookbook Sauce. Simmer 30 minutes or until chops are tender. Serve with hot cooked rice.

DO-AHEAD CORN RELISH. For 2 cups, combine 15-ounce can Italian Cookbook Sauce with ¾ cup drained whole kernel corn, ¼ cup finely chopped celery, 2 tablespoons finely chopped green pepper, 3 tablespoons finely chopped green onion, ⅛ teaspoon garlic salt, ¼ teaspoon salt, ⅛ teaspoon pepper, 1 teaspoon Worcestershire sauce, 5 or 6 drops hot pepper sauce, 2 tablespoons lime juice and 1 tablespoon cornstarch. Bring to boil in saucepan over medium heat. Simmer gently 5 to 10 minutes, stirring often. Chill in refrigerator. Perks up steaks, hamburgers or hot dogs on a busy day.

CONTINENTAL HAM AND VEGETABLES
(makes 3 to 4 servings)

2 pared large potatoes	1 slice (¾ to 1 inch thick)
2 medium onions	precooked ham
2 cups water	16-ounce can Sweet 'n Sour
¼ teaspoon salt	Cookbook Sauce
1 teaspoon dry mustard	2 tablespoons melted butter

Cut potatoes and onions into ¼-inch slices. Place in large skillet with water, salt and mustard. Cover. Simmer 15 to 20 minutes or until potatoes are barely tender. Drain potato and onion slices. Brush both sides of ham with Sweet 'n Sour Sauce. Brown ham in butter in skillet 10 minutes on each side. Add remaining Sweet 'n Sour Sauce to potatoes and onions. Simmer, uncovered, 10 to 15 minutes, stirring occasionally. Place ham slice on warm serving platter. Serve, sliced, with potatoes and onions.

BUDGET BOOSTER. How can you cut down on ironing? Get those permanent-press sheets, shirts and blouses. No way with your household allowance? Keep Contadina Cookbook Sauces in the cupboard. As an example, Creole, Italian and Sweet 'n Sour Sauces contain 17 special, or infrequently used, ingredients. Saves on the grocery bill—and on shelf space, too.

TOMATO VEGETABLE BAKE. For 4 to 6 servings, place one whole cooked medium cauliflower in 2-quart casserole. Combine 9-ounce package cooked, drained French-style green beans with ½ cup sliced onion, 1 cup drained whole kernel corn, 14½-ounce can stewed tomatoes, ⅛ teaspoon crushed rosemary and ½ teaspoon seasoned salt. Spoon mixture around cauliflower. Cover and bake in moderate oven (350°F.) 15 minutes. Remove cover. Sprinkle with ½ cup shredded Cheddar cheese. Bake, uncovered, 5 minutes longer. Serve with crisp bacon and chilled applesauce.

35-MINUTE SWEET AND SOUR MEATBALLS
(makes 4 to 6 servings)

1 pound lean ground beef	2 tablespoons oil
½ cup fine dry bread crumbs	1 cup sliced water chestnuts
1 egg	16-ounce can Sweet 'n Sour
¼ cup milk	Cookbook Sauce
¼ teaspoon garlic salt	4 cups hot cooked rice
½ teaspoon salt	

Combine ground beef, bread crumbs, egg, milk, garlic salt, and salt. Mix lightly but thoroughly. Shape into 12 meatballs. Brown 15 to 20 minutes in hot oil. Drain off fat. Add water chestnuts and Sweet 'n Sour Cookbook Sauce. Cover. Simmer 15 minutes. Place hot rice on serving platter. Spoon meatballs and sauce in center of rice. Serve at once.

SHORTCUT LASAGNE
(makes 6 to 8 servings)

1 pound ground chuck
1 teaspoon Italian seasoning
1 teaspoon sugar
2 cans Italian Cookbook Sauce
8 ounces cooked lasagne
   noodles

1 cup cottage cheese
1½ cups (6 ounces) shredded
   Mozzarella cheese
⅓ cup grated Parmesan
   cheese

Brown chuck in medium saucepan. Drain off fat. Add Italian seasoning, sugar and Italian Sauce. Simmer 10 minutes. Spread about ½ cup sauce in bottom of 12 x 7½ x 2-inch baking dish. Top with half of lasagne noodles. Combine cheeses. Top noodles with half of cheese and sauce mixtures. Repeat layers; end with sauce. Sprinkle generously with *additional* Parmesan cheese. Bake in moderate oven (350° F.) 30 to 35 minutes or until bubbly.

TUNA SWEET 'N SOUR
(makes 2 to 3 servings)

16-ounce can Sweet 'n Sour
   Cookbook Sauce
1 cup (6 to 7-ounce can)
   drained flaked tuna

½ cup finely chopped
   celery
Hot toasted chow mein
   noodles

Combine Sweet 'n Sour Sauce, tuna and celery in saucepan. Heat 10 to 15 minutes, stirring often. Serve over hot chow mein noodles. Fresh fruit, topped with sherbet, tea, and there's a sudden lunch for an unexpected guest.

15-MINUTE ITALIAN BEEF SANDWICHES
(makes 4 servings)

¾ pound thinly sliced
   cooked beef, ham or pork
15-ounce can Italian
   Cookbook Sauce

1 tablespoon brown sugar
1 teaspoon Italian seasoning
4 sourdough, onion or
   French rolls

Simmer meat slices, Italian Sauce, brown sugar and Italian seasoning in uncovered saucepan 15 minutes. Slice rolls in half. Baste with sauce. Arrange hot meat slices on bottom roll half. Spoon sauce over meat and top with second roll half.

Jiffy cooking

Remember the old line, "My mother told me there'd be days like this"? It turns out to be true, doesn't it? There are days when you can't seem to get the whole family together for a meal. There are days when the work piles up so that mealtime has arrived before you know it, and there you are with nothing to put on the table. There are days when the five you planned on for lunch have mysteriously multiplied to a dozen when lunch time comes around. There are days—but why go on? You don't need a lecture, you need help! On days like those, try some of the Jiffy Cooking ideas that follow. Who knows, you may even find that you have some time for yourself!

STRAWBERRY STOP for the after-school crowd. Just mix a glass of homogenized milk and a tablespoon of strawberry jam with a rotary beater or mixer. Serve it in a chilled glass or tall mug. It's energizing but doesn't spoil appetites.

OLIVE CHEESE NUT DIP FOR STUDYING SNACK. For 2 cups of snack, beat 2 cups cottage cheese with electric or rotary-type beater until creamy. Add ½ cup drained chopped ripe olives, ¼ cup chopped nuts, ¼ cup mayonnaise, ¼ teaspoon garlic salt and ¼ teaspoon salt. Mix well. Refrigerate and leave crackers or chips nearby.

CRISSCROSS PEANUT BUTTER COOKIES
(makes about 4 dozen cookies)

½ cup margarine	1 egg
1 cup peanut butter	⅓ cup buttermilk
½ teaspoon vanilla	1½ cups sifted flour
½ cup granulated sugar	1 teaspoon baking powder
½ cup firmly packed brown sugar	½ teaspoon baking soda
	½ teaspoon salt

Blend margarine, peanut butter, vanilla, sugars and egg until light and fluffy. Add buttermilk; mix well. Stir dry ingredients together

44

and add to margarine mixture. Blend until smooth. Drop from spoon to buttered baking sheet. Flatten cookies with floured fork tines in crisscross pattern. Bake in moderate oven (350° F.) 15 to 20 minutes. Place cookies on racks for cooling; store in tightly covered jar.

JIFFY SNACK HINT. Remember that those cookie-baker helpers eat almost as much dough as cookies. Better have a batch of Crisscross Peanut Butter Cookies in the freezer, just in case two dozen of the batch never get baked!

PIRATES' GROG
(makes 2 servings)

¼ cup chocolate syrup
1 pint coffee ice cream
½ teaspoon cinnamon
¾ cup homogenized milk

Spoon 2 tablespoons chocolate syrup in each of 2 12-ounce glasses. Place ice cream, cinnamon and milk in blender. Cover and blend at low speed 15 seconds. Stir. Blend 15 seconds at low speed. Pour ice cream mixture on top of chocolate syrup in glasses. Top with chocolate curls, if desired.

Combined with sufficient rest and exercise, proper food keeps energy up, supplies the body's daily needs, keeps skin clear, hair shining, eyes bright and bones strong. Proteins, carbohydrates, fats, minerals and vitamins in foods are the body's building blocks to better health. There's no need to make nutrition a complicated subject. Just think of each food in terms of what it contributes to better health. It's the GO, GROW AND GLOW "no-nonsense" nutrition course, for *every* member of the family.

FOODS TO GO ON: Carbohydrates and fats. Carbohydrates, or sugars such as lactose or sucrose, provide quick energy. Chase away the tired or "letdown" feeling with a glass of milk, orange juice, bananas, cereal with milk, or dried fruits. Fats supply energy, but more slowly. They can be stored in the body as a fuel reserve. Butter, oils and egg yolk are almost completely fat foods. Pork, avocado and nuts also have a high fat content.

FOODS TO GROW ON: Proteins. Protein is derived from the Greek word meaning "first," and protein is of first importance to good health. A new supply every day takes care of wear, tear and body repair. Put plenty of protein from eggs, meat, fish, poultry and milk into meals for that son who seems to be a size larger overnight.

FOODS TO GLOW ON: Minerals and vitamins. The list of minerals and vitamins needed by the body is a long one. Some people say it sounds like a combination of a miner's expedition and alphabet soup!

The body needs a wide variety of minerals and vitamins for the GLOW-ing look, a general feeling of well-being and good health. The "alphabet soup" group guards against small infections, provides protection against disease and promotes growth. Don't overlook vitamins. Members of the British Navy didn't get enough aboard ship, and suffered from scurvy. When limes were made a part of every day's meals, the scurvy was corrected, and that's how British sailors came to be called "limeys." Put plenty of fruits, enriched cereals, green and yellow vegetables in the family meals every day.

BACKYARD CHILI AND FRANKS
(makes 14 servings)

2 pounds ground chuck
2 cups chopped onions
¼ teaspoon pepper
4 teaspoons salt
2 tablespoons chili powder
¼ cup flour

2 tablespoons brown sugar
1 cup chili sauce
6 cups canned chili beans
2 cups (1 pint) sour cream
3 pounds broiled frankfurters
2 dozen frankfurter buns

Brown chuck in Dutch oven or 7 or 8-quart saucepan. Add onion and seasonings. Cook onions until tender. Add flour, brown sugar and chili sauce. Mix well. Add chili beans and cook over low heat until thickened, stirring constantly. Stir in sour cream. Heat to serving temperature. Serve over frankfurters on toasted frankfurter buns.

MANICURE SAVER. With or without a dishwasher pots and pans must be done —even when you have a brand-new manicure! Save chipped nails by holding your plastic or abrasive pot cleaner with a clothespin.

COOKIE CREAM LOAF FOR THE BACK-TO-SCHOOL CROWD
(this will serve 12 to 14 hungry ones)

2 cups crushed chocolate wafers (or crème-filled chocolate cookies)

½ cup chopped pecans
⅓ cup butter or margarine
½ gallon ice cream

Mix chocolate wafer crumbs with pecans and melted butter or margarine. Divide crumb mixture into 4 equal parts of about ½ cup each. Divide ½ gallon ice cream into 3 equal parts. Cut into slices. Line 9 x 5 x 3-inch pan with foil. Beginning with crumb mixture, alternate layers of crumbs and ice cream. End with crumb mixture. Freeze 1 to 2 hours. Unmold from pan and remove foil. Top with chocolate or marshmallow sauce and chopped nuts.

EVERYONE COOKS HIS OWN BEEF FONDUE
Allow about ½ pound beef sirloin or tenderloin per person. Cut into ½ to ¾-inch cubes. Provide everyone in the family with wooden-handled fondue forks or skewers. (You'll find

many of the fondue forks have a color dot on them, so that each person can "color key" his own.) Fill your fondue pot half full of hot vegetable oil; heat to just below boiling. Place on heater. Each person puts a cube of meat on his fork, dips it in hot fat until the meat is cooked, then uses a Curried Horseradish or Nippy Chili Sauce for it.

CURRIED HORSERADISH SAUCE
(makes 1 cup)

1 tablespoon butter	1 teaspoon curry powder
1 tablespoon flour	2 teaspoons horseradish
1 cup half and half	½ teaspoon seasoned salt

Melt butter in saucepan. Add flour and blend until smooth. Slowly add half and half, stirring constantly. Cook over medium heat until sauce thickens, or about 10 minutes. Remove from heat. Add remaining ingredients. (Add a dash of seasoned pepper, if desired.) Stir until sauce is smooth, and serve with Beef Fondue.

NIPPY CHILI SAUCE. For about 1½ cups, blend 1 cup sour cream, 1 tablespoon chili sauce, ¼ teaspoon seasoned pepper, 1 tablespoon grated onion, ½ teaspoon seasoned salt and 2 teaspoons hot taco sauce in small saucepan. Heat to serving temperature. Do not boil. Serve warm with Beef Fondue.

49

EASY-DOES-IT HAM LOAF WITH
HORSERADISH SAUCE
(makes 6 to 8 servings)

1 pound ground smoked ham	½ cup finely chopped onion
1 pound ground fresh pork	¼ teaspoon cayenne pepper
1 cup cottage cheese	¼ teaspoon paprika
2 slightly beaten eggs	¼ teaspoon crushed rosemary
⅓ cup fine dry bread crumbs	

Combine all ingredients in large bowl. Mix gently but thoroughly.
Press meat mixture into 8½ x 4½ x 2½-inch loaf pan. Bake in
moderate oven (350° F.) 1½ hours. Drain off excess fat. Place
on warm serving platter and serve with Fluffy Horseradish Sauce.

FLUFFY HORSERADISH SAUCE. Makes about 1 cup. Beat
½ cup all-purpose cream until stiff. Combine ¼ teaspoon
salt, ⅛ teaspoon cayenne, ¼ teaspoon Worcestershire sauce,
2 teaspoons horseradish and 1 teaspoon prepared mustard.
Mix well. Fold horseradish mixture into whipped cream. Serve
with Ham Loaf.

SUPER SPINACH SALAD
(makes 6 to 8 servings)

¼ pound washed, dried chilled fresh spinach	⅓ cup sliced green onions
	2 chopped hard-cooked eggs
½ cup crumbled crisply fried bacon	1 cup cottage cheese
	Favorite salad dressing

Tear spinach leaves into bite-sized pieces. Combine spinach, bacon,
onions, eggs and cottage cheese. Toss together lightly but thoroughly. Chill until serving time, then toss with a favorite salad
dressing.

QUICK SHRIMP-AVOCADO DIP
(makes about 2½ cups)

2 ripe avocados	¼ teaspoon salt
1 cup sour cream	1 cup cooked chopped shrimp
2 tablespoons chili sauce	

Remove skin and pits from avocados. Mash with fork. Add sour
cream, chili sauce and salt. Fold in shrimp, then serve with potato
chips, corn chips or crackers.

50

PATIO CARROT AND RAISIN SALAD
(makes 6 to 8 servings)

2 3-ounce packages orange
  gelatin
2 cups hot water
1½ cups sour cream
⅓ cup mayonnaise

⅔ cup grated carrots
½ cup seedless raisins
1⅔ cups crushed pineapple
  with syrup

Dissolve gelatin in hot water in medium bowl. Chill to consistency of unbeaten egg whites. Add sour cream and mayonnaise. Blend until smooth. Stir in remaining ingredients. Pour into 5-cup mold. Chill until set (about 2 hours). Unmold and serve on platter garnished with lettuce or watercress.

SIMPLE SUMMER SALAD
(makes 4 to 6 servings)

2 7-ounce cans drained, flaked
  tuna
1 cup thinly sliced celery
½ cup drained, sliced ripe
  olives
1 cup drained pineapple
  tidbits

¾ cup toasted chopped nuts
1 cup pineapple yogurt
1 tablespoon mayonnaise
1 teaspoon seasoned salt
½ teaspoon ground ginger

Combine tuna, celery, olives, pineapple and nuts in bowl. Blend remaining ingredients and beat until smooth. Pour over tuna-fruit mixture. Mix thoroughly. Chill, then serve on lettuce-lined platter.

WINTER FRUIT COCKTAIL BROIL
(makes 8 servings)

2⅔ cups drained fruit
  cocktail (or leftover mixed
  fruit)

2 cups (1 pint) sour cream
½ cup light brown sugar
¼ teaspoon cinnamon

Spoon fruit into 8 custard cups. Spread sour cream over fruit. Combine brown sugar and cinnamon. Sprinkle top of each cup with sugar mixture to cover sour cream completely. Place custard cups on cookie sheet. Broil 4 inches from heat 3 minutes or until sugar is bubbly and crusty.

Last-minute meals

Unexpected company for dinner needn't send you into a panic. Do a quick review of your planned-on menu to see what you can change here, add to there, pretty up a little. Add cool mugs of soup for starters, a special Tomato (salad) Trick for another course. Or turn the meat you were going to use as beef patties into Ground Beef Stroganoff in Minutes, or the green beans you were going to serve simply buttered into Frankly Fancy Green Bean Puff. Whatever tonight's menu was going to be, you can stretch a little here, dress up a little there, and you'll have a meal you'll be proud to serve.

FRANKLY FANCY GREEN BEAN PUFF
(makes 8 to 10 servings)

4 cups cooked drained
  French-style green beans
2 14½-ounce cans well-drained
  sliced baby tomatoes
Parmesan cheese
3 tablespoons minced onion
2 tablespoons melted butter
3 tablespoons flour
1⅓ cups milk

¾ cup shredded sharp
  Cheddar cheese
3 well-beaten egg yolks
1 teaspoon sugar
¼ teaspoon garlic salt
⅛ teaspoon white pepper
¼ teaspoon salt
3 egg whites

Arrange beans in well-buttered 13 x 9 x 2-inch baking dish. Place all but 12 tomato slices on beans. Sprinkle with Parmesan. Sauté onion in butter 1 to 2 minutes in saucepan. Stir in flour. Gradually add milk. Cook over medium heat until thickened, stirring constantly. Stir in Cheddar until melted. Remove from heat; add egg yolks, sugar, garlic salt, pepper and salt. Beat until blended. Beat egg whites until stiff. Fold into sauce. Pour evenly over tomatoes and beans. Top with remaining 12 tomato slices. Bake in moderate oven (350° F.) 20 to 30 minutes or until set and lightly browned.

WATERMELON WAIKIKI
(makes 6 to 8 servings)

½ of 13-inch watermelon
3 cups honeydew melon balls
2 cups sweetened sliced
  fresh peaches

1½ cups sweetened
  strawberry halves
1 quart raspberry ice cream
Mint leaves

Notch edges of watermelon, if desired. Remove seeds. Use large
end of melon baller to make 4 cups watermelon balls. Scrape out
remaining melon to form bowl from watermelon shell. Combine
melon balls, peaches and strawberries. Mix gently. Spoon into
watermelon shell. Chill until serving time. Just before serving,
place scoops of ice cream on top of fruit. Garnish with mint leaves,
and serve at once.

**NO TIME TO MAKE ALL THOSE LITTLE
MELON BALLS? Remove watermelon and honeydew in sections. Chop into bite-sized pieces with
silver knife.**

QUICK-TO-FIX VEGETABLE CHOWDER
(makes about 2 quarts)

4 cups peeled, diced raw
  potatoes
10-ounce package mixed
  frozen vegetables
2½ cups water
1 teaspoon salt

4 slices bacon
½ cup chopped onion
¾ cup chopped celery
1⅔ cups *undiluted*
  Velvetized evaporated milk
¼ cup fine cracker crumbs

Place potatoes and mixed vegetables in saucepan. Add water and
salt. Cover. Cook over medium heat until potatoes are tender
(about 20 minutes). Do not drain. Cut bacon into small pieces.
Fry until partially cooked. Add onion and celery. Continue cooking until onions are transparent and celery tender. Mix bacon,
onions and celery with potato-vegetable mixture. Add evaporated
milk. Heat to serving temperature, but *do not boil.* Just before
serving, stir in cracker crumbs.

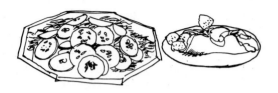

GINGER-CHEESE CHEWS
(makes 4 to 5 dozen . . . for after-swimming)

1 cup cottage cheese
½ cup milk
1 14-ounce package
  gingerbread mix

½ cup raisins
¾ cup chopped nuts

Beat cottage cheese in large bowl until smooth. Add milk. Slowly add gingerbread mix and beat well. Stir in raisins and ½ *cup nuts.* Drop by heaping teaspoonfuls on buttered baking sheet. Sprinkle with remaining chopped nuts. Bake in moderate oven (350° F.) 15 minutes. Remove and cool on wire racks.

WHEN ALL ELSE FAILS, reach for those handy mixes. Make ginger cheese chews from gingerbread mix, or "dress up" leftovers, as below, with packaged Noodles Romanoff!

HAM AND CHEESE ROMANOFF
(makes 4 to 6 servings)

1 5¾-ounce package Noodles
  Romanoff
½ cup chopped onion
2 tablespoons butter or
  margarine
2 cups diced cooked ham

½ cup drained sliced
  mushrooms
1 cup cottage cheese
½ cup sour cream
¼ cup homogenized milk

Cook noodles according to package directions. Sauté onion in melted butter in large skillet until tender. Stir in ham, mushrooms and drained cooked noodles. Blend cottage cheese, sour cream, milk and Romanoff Sauce in small bowl. Add to ham mixture in skillet. Stir while heating to serving temperature, 5 to 10 minutes. Garnish with paprika and parsley, if desired.

54

GROUND BEEF STROGANOFF IN MINUTES
(makes 4 to 6 servings)

¾ cup chopped onion
2 tablespoons butter
1½ pounds ground chuck
1 minced clove garlic
2 tablespoons flour
3 tablespoons tomato paste
1 tablespoon prepared mustard

½ cup sliced mushrooms
1 teaspoon salt
¼ teaspoon pepper
1 tablespoon lemon juice
½ cup beef broth
1½ cups sour cream

Brown onion in butter until tender. Add ground chuck and garlic. Cook until meat is browned. Drain off fat. Sprinkle flour over beef; mix well. Add tomato paste, mustard, mushrooms, salt, pepper, lemon juice and beef broth. Simmer slowly, 5 minutes. Stir in sour cream. Heat to serving temperature and serve at once over cooked rice or noodles.

THE CLOCK STRIKES SIX AND FATHER'S NOT HOME? That's the way it goes, sometimes. Don't add the sour cream to Ground Beef Stroganoff until you are sure everyone is ready to eat!

29-MINUTE BEANS 'N' FRANKS IN A BOWL
(makes 6 to 8 servings)

½ cup chopped onion
⅓ cup chopped green pepper
3 tablespoons margarine
2 tablespoons flour
1⅔ cups *undiluted*
   Velvetized evaporated milk

⅔ cup water
2 cups canned baked beans
1 cup tomato sauce
1¼ teaspoons seasoned salt
3 coarsely chopped frankfurters

Sauté onion and green pepper in margarine in medium-sized saucepan until tender. Stir in flour. Slowly stir in evaporated milk. Add remaining ingredients. Stir to blend. Heat over low heat 20 minutes. Serve at once in mugs or bowls.

PINEAPPLE NUT SPREAD. Beat 2 cups cottage cheese with electric or rotary beater until creamy. Add ½ cup well-drained canned crushed pineapple, ¼ cup mayonnaise, 1 tablespoon lemon juice, ¼ cup chopped nuts, ¼ teaspoon salt, ¼ teaspoon ginger and 1 teaspoon sugar. Blend well. Serve on brown bread or crackers for an after-school snack.

TROPICAL TREAT. For 6 thirsty ones, combine ½ quart buttermilk and 2 cups pineapple juice. Chill. Just before the tribe comes home, add 2 8-ounce bottles ginger ale. Serve over ice cubes in tall glasses. Garnish with a bit of nutmeg.

LIMEADE SPARKLE
(makes 3 quarts)

2 6-ounce cans frozen limeade	½ cup sugar
1½ cups sliced fresh strawberries	3 cups ginger ale

Mix limeade according to label directions. Blend strawberries and sugar. Allow to stand ½ hour. Combine strawberry-sugar mixture with limeade; mix well. Just before serving, add ginger ale and pour over ice cubes.

Sudden soups

ZIPPY CHICKEN BROTH. For about 2 cups, combine 1 14-ounce can chicken broth, ½ cup tomato puree and 1 teaspoon Worcestershire sauce in pan. Heat to serving temperature.

TOMATO-ONION CUP. For about 2 cups or mugs of soup, combine 1 10½-ounce can onion soup, ½ cup tomato puree and ½ cup water in saucepan. Heat and serve.

PATIO POTATO SALAD
When you're expecting 6 hungry boys with double appetites

2 quarts diced cooked
  potatoes (4 to 6 potatoes)
⅔ cup finely chopped onion
⅔ cup chopped green pepper
1⅓ cups chopped sweet
  pickles
1⅓ cups chopped celery

1⅓ cups chopped radishes
10 to 12 hard-cooked eggs
4 teaspoons salt
⅛ teaspoon pepper
2 teaspoons prepared mustard
2 cups sour cream

Mix potatoes with onion, chopped green pepper, sweet pickles, celery and radishes in bowl. Chop eggs and add to potato mixture. Blend salt, pepper, mustard and sour cream. Spoon over potato mixture. Mix lightly. Cover salad and refrigerate at least 1 hour to blend flavors. Serve garnished with parsley, sliced hard-cooked eggs or tomatoes.

DO-IT-YOURSELF SANDWICH TRAY. Place cold cuts, cheese, buttered bread slices, celery, pickles and mustard on tray. Use paper cups, paper plates, and let the boys clean up!

HALIBUT HAWAIIAN
(makes about 4 servings)

2 pounds fresh or defrosted
  frozen halibut steaks
2 teaspoons seasoned salt
1 teaspoon pepper
¼ teaspoon thyme
2 tablespoons butter or
  margarine

¾ cup sour cream
2 cups drained canned
  grapefruit sections
¼ cup flaked coconut

Place halibut in lightly buttered 12 x 7½ x 2-inch baking dish. Sprinkle with seasoned salt, pepper and thyme. Dot with butter. Bake in moderate oven (350° F.) 20 to 25 minutes until halibut flakes lightly. Remove from oven. Heat broiler. Spread sour cream over halibut. Arrange grapefruit sections on top of sour cream. Sprinkle with coconut. Broil 3 to 5 minutes or until coconut is golden and sour cream bubbly.

LIGHT AND TENDER OMELET
(makes 6 servings)

8 strips bacon
8 egg yolks
½ teaspoon salt
⅛ teaspoon pepper
1 cup cottage cheese

½ cup shredded Cheddar
cheese
8 egg whites
2 tablespoons bacon fat

Fry bacon until crisp. Drain and break into small pieces. Save 2 tablespoons bacon fat. Beat egg yolks, salt and pepper until thick and lemon-colored. Add cottage cheese, Cheddar and bacon. Beat egg whites until stiff, but not dry. Fold into egg yolk mixture. Heat bacon fat in 10-inch skillet. Pour in egg mixture. Cook over low heat about 5 minutes or until bottom is lightly browned. Bake in moderate oven (350° F.) 20 to 25 minutes or until top is dry and knife inserted in center comes out clean.

OMELET WITH AN ITALIAN TOUCH. When serving your Light and Tender Omelet, top with warm Italian Cookbook Sauce. Gives a new flavor touch to eggs.

CUCUMBER SHRIMP CUP
(makes 8 to 10 servings)

2 cups shredded unpeeled
cucumber
1½ cups sour cream
¼ cup homogenized milk
1 teaspoon Worcestershire
sauce
¼ cup finely chopped chives
1 tablespoon white wine
vinegar

½ teaspoon salt
¼ teaspoon pepper
⅛ teaspoon tarragon
2 tablespoons finely
chopped sweet pickle
1⅔ cups drained, small
deveined canned shrimp
Finely chopped parsley

Combine cucumber, sour cream, milk, Worcestershire, chives, vinegar, salt, pepper and tarragon in medium bowl. Mix well. Chill thoroughly. Just before serving, stir in sweet pickle and shrimp. Spoon into small cups or bowls and sprinkle with parsley. Serve as an appetizer with crisp crackers or Melba toast.

THREE-IN-ONE SANDWICHES GRILLED IN MINUTES

1 cup cottage cheese
½ cup well-drained canned
   crushed pineapple
12 slices sandwich bread

6 thin slices American cheese
6 thin slices ham
Mustard
½ cup melted butter

Preheat griddle to 300° F. or use large skillet. Combine cottage cheese and pineapple. Blend well. Place 1 slice cheese on each of 6 bread slices. Spread about ¼ cup cheese-pineapple mixture over cheese. Top with ham slice. Spread remaining bread slices with mustard and place over ham. Butter both sides of sandwiches. Toast on griddle or in frying pan about 2 minutes on each side. Ready to serve—6 sandwiches in minutes.

Fresh tomato tricks

VEGETABLE TOMATO FANS. Combine 2 cups cottage cheese, 2 teaspoons grated onion, ¼ cup minced green pepper, ¼ cup minced radishes, 1 teaspoon seasoned salt, ½ teaspoon salt and ¼ teaspoon seasoned pepper. Blend well and chill. Use as stuffing for tomatoes. To make tomato fans, wash and dry chilled, firm fresh tomatoes. Remove cores. Make three vertical slits in each tomato, cutting within an inch of the bottom. Spread tomato apart gently. Place filling in slits and serve on chilled lettuce.

TOMATO CARTWHEELS. Combine ½ cup mashed blue cheese, 2 cups cottage cheese, ¼ teaspoon salt, ½ teaspoon seasoned salt, a few grains garlic salt and ¼ cup finely chopped green pepper. Blend well and chill. Wash and dry chilled tomatoes. Remove cores, then cut a thin slice from tomato top. Scoop out pulp carefully so that tomato skin does not break. Fill with cheese mixture. Cut tomatoes into half-inch slices. Serve on platter with cold cuts, hot biscuits and iced tea.

MANHATTAN CLAM CHOWDER
(makes 2 quarts)

¼ pound diced salt pork
1 large diced onion
1 cup diced raw carrots
1 cup diced celery
3½ cups Italian Style
 tomatoes
1 teaspoon salt

¼ teaspoon pepper
3 cups minced or chopped
 clams
1 cup clam liquid
2 cups water
½ cup cracker crumbs

Brown salt pork in large saucepan. Sauté onion with pork until clear. Add carrots, celery, tomatoes and seasonings. Stir to break up tomatoes. Drain clams; save 1 cup liquid. Add clam liquid and water to vegetables. Simmer, uncovered, 1 hour. Add clams. Continue cooking 5 to 10 minutes. Sprinkle with cracker crumbs. Serve at once.

WINTER EMERGENCY SHELF
in the cupboard or freezer

Frozen mixed vegetables
Cookie mix or refrigerator
 cookies
Velvetized evaporated milk
Noodle mixes
Sliced canned mushrooms
Chopped pimiento

Cookbook Sauces (for leftover
 ham, beef or chicken)
Tomato sauce
Canned beef consommé or
 bouillon cubes
Canned fruits for sudden salads
Extra crackers for soup suppers

SUMMER EMERGENCY SHELF

Sandwich bread
Cold cuts
Frozen fruit juices,
 lemonade or limeade
Ground chuck (wrapped
 properly, labeled and dated)
Frozen soups

Fruit-flavored gelatin
Instant Breakfast (for the
 "sleep-in" crowd)
Sweet 'n Sour Cookbook Sauce
 for patio cooking
Chicken broth
Soft drinks

Vacation time— for everyone

At the mountains, the shore, the cottage, the lake or on a cross-country jaunt, you're sometimes expected to come up with mealtime magic . . . miles away from your own convenient kitchen, range and refrigerator.

PACK LIGHT. Take wash-and-wear shirts, sweaters, slacks and skirts. Pack plenty of paper plates, napkins and cups for no-dishwashing days. Don't forget to have a variety of Instant Breakfast flavors, Instant nonfat dry milk and jars of Coffee-mate.

KEEP VACATION CHORES to a minimum. Cover cooking pans and fish-frying skillet bottom with foil to prevent them from being blackened over the campfire.

BREAKFAST FOR THE EARLY-BIRD FISHERMEN while you sleep. Put the vacuum bottle, instant coffee, Coffee-mate and envelopes of Instant Breakfast together in the kitchen. Leave a note, reminding your men to make their coffee and take a quart of milk along to the fishing spot.

SAVE bacon drippings in a clean, dry covered can or jar for frying the fishermen's catch.

MIX Instant nonfat dry milk according to label directions after dinner each night. Refrigerate it, so there's a morning supply for drinking, cereal topping or cooking.

USE YOUR MAGIC WAND AT DESSERT TIME. Reach for the Coffee-mate for a Sudden Custard, or cake icing for those who like *anything* . . . as long as it's chocolate!

SUDDEN CUSTARD
(makes 6 servings)

½ cup non-dairy
  coffee creamer
2 cups hot water
4 eggs

¼ cup sugar
¼ teaspoon salt
1 teaspoon vanilla
Nutmeg

Combine non-dairy coffee creamer and hot water. Add remaining ingredients, except nutmeg. Beat well with rotary beater. Pour into six 6-ounce custard cups. Sprinkle with nutmeg. Place in pan about 2 inches deep. Pour hot water around cups to 1-inch depth. Bake' in moderate oven (350° F.) 40 to 45 minutes or until knife inserted in center of custard comes out clean. Remove from water and cool on rack at room temperature. Top with sugared fresh berries from a nearby fruit stand.

WEEPY CUSTARDS? Remember to place custard cups in water, as the recipe directs. The silver knife test tells you when custards are done. If you've followed these custard clues carefully and still have problems, leave a note for the cottage landlord to have the oven temperature checked.

CHOCOLATE ICING FOR COTTAGE COOKING
(makes icing for 13 x 9 x 2-inch cake)

1 6-ounce package
  semisweet chocolate
  pieces
¼ cup butter or margarine

2¼ cups sifted
  confectioners sugar
¼ cup liquefied non-
  dairy coffee creamer

Melt chocolate pieces and butter in saucepan over low heat, stirring frequently. Cool thoroughly. Alternately blend in sugar and liquid non-dairy coffee creamer. Beat well to spreading consistency, and top cake .

AFTER-SUNNING ORANGE COOLER
(makes 1 cooler)

1 cup milk
1 envelope Vanilla
   Instant Breakfast

3 tablespoons frozen orange
   juice concentrate

Combine milk and Instant Breakfast mix in blender or screw-top jar. Blend or shake for a few seconds until powder is dissolved. Add frozen orange juice concentrate gradually, beating or shaking to prevent curdling. Mix until frothy and light.

AWAY-FROM-HOME CHEESE SAUCE
(makes about 1½ cups)

2 tablespoons butter or
   margarine
2 tablespoons flour
¼ teaspoon salt
Few grains pepper

1 cup water
¼ cup non-dairy coffee
   creamer
1 cup grated sharp Cheddar
   cheese

Melt butter in saucepan. Add flour, salt and pepper. Stir until smooth. Add water, then stir until well blended. Add non-dairy coffee creamer. Cook until thickened. Add Cheddar and stir over low heat until cheese melts. Serve over hot cooked fresh vegetables. (It's good on hamburgers, too.)

BUTTERSCOTCH SUNDAE SAUCE
(makes about 1 cup)

1 6-ounce package
   butterscotch pieces
⅓ cup chopped nuts
¼ teaspoon nutmeg
¼ teaspoon allspice

¼ cup non-dairy coffee
   creamer
⅓ cup water
2 tablespoons sugar

Combine all ingredients in small saucepan. Cook over low heat, stirring constantly until butterscotch pieces are melted. Serve warm or cool over ice cream, leftover cake slices. Top with chopped nuts, if desired.

65

FUDGE FOR A RAINY VACATION DAY
(makes 2 pounds)

¼ cup butter
½ cup liquid Coffee-mate
2 cups sugar
½ teaspoon salt
1 cup marshmallow crème

2 cups semisweet
  chocolate chips
½ cup chopped nuts
1 teaspoon vanilla

Combine butter, liquid Coffee-mate, sugar and salt in 2-quart saucepan. Heat to boiling. Cook 6 minutes, stirring constantly. (Start timing when mixture starts to bubble around edges of pan.) Remove from heat. Add remaining ingredients. Stir vigorously 1 minute until chocolate and marshmallow melt. Pour into 8-inch-square buttered pan. Cool in refrigerator. Cut into squares.

> BE SURE to pack fun-makers for rainy days . . . poster paints, jigsaw puzzles, dominoes or playing cards. And don't forget an extra jar of Coffee-mate. It's not only a low-calorie coffee creamer, but a lifesaver on rainy days. Read the label—there are easy directions for mixing it with water. Then stir up a batch of fudge or a meat loaf for around-the-fire fun.

CAMPERS' MEAT LOAF
(makes 8 servings)

2 pounds ground chuck
1 teaspoon salt
¼ teaspoon pepper
2 eggs

½ cup soft bread crumbs
½ cup liquid Coffee-mate
½ cup chopped onion
½ teaspoon crushed basil

Combine all ingredients. Mix gently but thoroughly. Place in 9 x 5 x 3-inch loaf pan. Bake in moderate oven (375° F.) 60 minutes. Allow to stand 5 to 10 minutes before serving.

Summertime

The livin' isn't necessarily easy when summertime comes around—but with a bit of planning, a little forethought, plus a determination on your part not be a household drudge, the livin' can be easier.

Do-aheads are summertime lifesavers. Cook in the cool of the day. On rainy days, spend a little extra time in the kitchen preparing food that can go into the freezer against days when you'll want to be out in the sun.

Prepare yourself for the teen-agers with Summer Coolers and Lots-of-Lemon Wafers, and gear up for Hospitality Jr., with ideas on page 73. On page 74, there are lots of Ice Cream, Cake and Cookie Capers to keep the little people happy.

Serve backyard dinners with Sauce for Backyard Buns or fancier Orientalburgers. Keep a cupboard full of Cookbook Sauces to brighten an omelet, vary vegetables, or shortcut hot summer days' cooking.

Summer is a good time to learn to shop well and wisely. REMEMBER the shopping list? Without one, it's easy to get carried away and purchase things you don't need, but forget the necessary detergent.

CHECK the refrigerator for leftover meats or cooked vegetables that can be used for hearty salads, soups or casseroles.

LEARN to be a label reader. Fruits are packed in a heavy, medium or light syrup. Buy the less expensive mushroom pieces if you are planning to slice or chop.

SHOP early in the day so that you can take time to compare costs of frozen, canned or fresh fruits and vegetables.

8 GREAT TOMATO MEN SAUCE FOR BACKYARD BUNS
(makes 8 servings)

1 tablespoon butter	⅔ cup tomato paste
½ cup chopped onion	1 cup tomato sauce
⅓ cup chopped green pepper	2 teaspoons seasoned salt
⅓ cup chopped celery	½ teaspoon seasoned pepper
1½ pounds ground chuck	½ teaspoon chili powder

Melt butter in large frying pan. Cook vegetables in butter until tender. Add chuck. Brown over medium heat. Add remaining ingredients. Stir until well blended. Cook 10 minutes. Serve over toasted hamburger buns and garnish with cheese strips, if desired.

. . . "Fancy up" hamburgers for last-minute guests with

ORIENTALBURGERS FOR 4

½ pound ground chuck	2 teaspoons soy sauce
½ pound ground pork	½ teaspoon salt
1 slightly beaten egg	¼ teaspoon ground ginger
½ cup chopped water chestnuts	4 green pepper rings, ½-inch thick
2 teaspoons grated lemon rind	1 14½-ounce can sliced baby tomatoes

Mix all ingredients except pepper rings and tomatoes lightly but thoroughly. Shape into 4 patties ½ inch thick. Bake on broiler pan in moderate oven (350° F.) 15 minutes. Turn. Bake another 20 minutes. Place each patty on pepper ring. Drain tomatoes, save liquid. Top hamburgers with 12 slices tomato; save remaining slices for sauce. Bake 5 minutes longer. Serve with Oriental Sauce and rice.

FOR ORIENTAL SAUCE, chop leftover tomato slices. Blend 1 tablespoon cornstarch, 1 tablespoon corn syrup, 1 tablespoon soy sauce, 1 tablespoon vinegar and 2 tablespoons sugar in saucepan. Slowly add tomato liquid and chopped tomatoes. Bring mixture to boil over medium heat. Stir constantly. Boil 3 minutes, stirring occasionally.

COOL CHICKEN SOUP, FAR EAST. For 1 quart, combine 1 tablespoon cornstarch with 2 teaspoons curry powder. Measure 3½ cups chicken broth. Add small amount of broth to cornstarch-curry mixture to make a thin paste. Mix paste with chicken broth and 1 tablespoon grated onion in saucepan. Mix well. Heat to boiling. Stir constantly 2 to 3 minutes. Cool to lukewarm. Stir in 1 cup sour cream. Chill well. Serve in chilled bowls or mugs garnished with chopped chives.

EASY-ON-THE-BUDGET TUNA AND NOODLES
AU GRATIN
(makes 4 servings)

¼ cup margarine	3 cups hot cooked noodles
¼ cup flour	⅓ cup finely chopped onion
½ teaspoon salt	¼ cup finely chopped
¼ teaspoon pepper	green pepper
2 cups milk	2 tablespoons chopped
½ cup grated Parmesan cheese	pimiento
1 cup cottage cheese	Paprika
1 cup drained flaked tuna	

Melt margarine in saucepan over low heat. Add flour, salt and pepper. Blend well. Gradually add milk. Cook over low heat until mixture is thickened and smooth. Remove from heat. Add Parmesan and cottage cheese. Stir until well blended. Mix tuna, noodles, onion, green pepper and pimiento in bowl. Add cheese sauce. Mix well, then pour into 2-quart casserole. Sprinkle with paprika. Bake in moderate oven (350° F.) 20 to 25 minutes. Serve at once.

EVERYONE HAVING A VACATION BUT YOU, MOM? Early in the day, when it's cool, make Potato and Ham Picnic Salad. The recipe is on page 78. Cut up vegetables for a relish tray and place them in plastic bags. Retreat to the beauty parlor, shop or find a friend for "adult talk." When you arrive home, take dinner from the refrigerator.

Six summer coolers

(Ideas for just *one* thirsty one)

GRAPE PINEAPPLE SODA. Pour ½ to ¾ cup grape juice into a tall glass. Add 2 scoops of pineapple sherbet. Add ½ to ¾ cup lemon-lime beverage. Stir. Top with whipped cream, if desired. Garnish with cherry.

CHOCOLATE LIME FIZZ. Pour ¼ cup chocolate syrup into a tall glass. Add ½ cup cold milk. Mix well. Add 2 scoops lime sherbet and ½ to ¾ cup sparkling water. Stir. Top with whipped cream and garnish with a mint leaf.

PINEAPPLE RASPBERRY FLOAT. Pour ½ to ¾ cup pineapple juice into a tall glass. Add 2 scoops raspberry sherbet. Add ½ to ¾ cup sparkling water. Stir and serve topped with whipped cream and a cherry.

HAWAIIAN COOLER. Place ¾ cup fruit punch in tall glass. Add 2 scoops pineapple sherbet. Add ¾ cup lemon-lime beverage. Stir. Serve topped with whipped cream, pineapple chunks and a cherry.

BERRY GOOD BUTTERMILK. Place ¼ to ½ cup crushed, thawed frozen berries (or the same amount of sweetened crushed fresh berries) in tall glass. Add cold buttermilk. Stir and serve garnished with a mint leaf.

RASPBERRY SHERBET SHAKE. Place 2 scoops raspberry sherbet in tall glass. Add a small amount of cold milk. Blend until smooth. Add another ½ cup milk and ¼ to ⅓ cup raspberry juice (from defrosted frozen or mashed fresh berries). Add ⅓ cup sparkling water. Stir and serve topped with whipped cream and berries.

LOTS-OF-LEMON WAFERS
(makes about 5 dozen)

1 cup margarine
1½ cups sugar, divided
1 egg
½ teaspoon vanilla
½ teaspoon lemon extract
2¼ cups sifted flour
1 teaspoon baking powder
½ teaspoon salt
¼ teaspoon soda
⅓ cup *undiluted* Velvetized
   evaporated milk
1 tablespoon grated
   lemon rind

Cream margarine with *1 cup* sugar until light and fluffy. Beat in egg, vanilla and lemon extract. Sift dry ingredients together. Add dry ingredients to sugar mixture alternately with evaporated milk. Chill at least 2 hours. Roll rounded teaspoonfuls into balls. Mix remaining ½ cup sugar and lemon rind. Roll balls in sugar. Place 2 inches apart on baking sheets. Bake in moderate oven (350° F.) 8 to 10 minutes or until cookies are lightly browned around edges. Cool on cake racks.

SPICY CHOCOLATE CAKE SQUARES
(makes 12 servings)

2 cups sifted flour
2 teaspoons baking powder
½ teaspoon soda
¼ teaspoon salt
1 teaspoon cloves
2 teaspoons nutmeg
4 teaspoons cinnamon
⅓ cup cocoa
1 cup margarine
2 cups sugar
3 eggs
1½ cups mashed potatoes
⅔ cup *undiluted* Velvetized
   evaporated milk
⅓ cup water
1 tablespoon vinegar
1 cup raisins
1 cup chopped nuts

Line bottom of 13 x 9 x 2-inch baking pan with wax paper. Sift flour, baking powder, soda, salt, cloves, nutmeg, cinnamon and cocoa together. Cream margarine and sugar. Add eggs. Beat until light and fluffy. Beat in potatoes. Mix evaporated milk, water and vinegar. Alternately add milk-vinegar mixture and sifted dry ingredients. Mix until well blended. Stir in raisins and nuts. Pour into pan. Bake in moderate oven (350° F.) 50 to 55 minutes or until toothpick inserted in center comes out clean. Cool and serve cut in squares.

Hospitality, Jr.

It's every woman's dream to have a backyard or family room full of well-mannered little guests. That's a dream, for sure, but you'll have fewer party nightmares if you:

PLAN a party around activities. The restless 8 and 10-year olds need a picnic, swim or, when the weather is bad, a movie.

REMOVE family treasures to a safe place. The youngsters do dash around tables, chairs and furniture at a rocketing speed.

SERVE simple food and lots of it. Hamburgers, hot dogs, ice cream and cake are winners every time.

Party plotting

LIGHTHEARTED PLACE CARDS. Insert white candles into small, colorful gum drops. Fasten gum drops to white cards and write each guest's name on a card in colored crayon.

PARTY CUT-OUTS. Keep small guests busy with surprise cut-outs they can take home. Use valentines, witches, turkeys or whatever is seasonal. Have plenty of paper doilies, colored paper, paste and blunt scissors (also plenty of soap and paper towels for soiled hands).

Ice cream, cake and cookie capers

ICE CREAM MOUNTAIN. Place small ice cream cones or cups around edge of large platter. Fill a bowl with scoops of several flavors of ice cream and place it in the center of the platter. Let each child select his own "very favorite one."

GINGERBREAD SCURRY. If you're suddenly showered with hungry ones, bake a cake or gingerbread mix in a loaf pan. (Remember to read those label directions for the proper pan size.) Serve scoops of ice cream over warm cake squares.

DO-IT-YOURSELF DECORATING. Place scoops of ice cream in coffee or soup mugs. Store in the freezer until serving time. Place colorful cake decorations, chocolate sauce, chopped nuts in individual bowls. Let each child do his own (ice cream) decorating.

KEEN CONES. Gently place two candy canes in sides of ice cream cone for "arms." Top with scoop of ice cream. Use bits of chocolate or gum drops for eyes and mouth. The hat is a cookie. Freeze until serving time.

MERRY-GO-ROUND. Spoon or scoop ice cream on paper plates. Parade animal crackers in a circle around the ice cream and top with maraschino cherry.

ICE CREAM CRUNCH. Combine ½ cup finely crushed cornflakes with ¼ cup finely chopped nuts. Roll scoops of ice cream in mixture. Serve plain or with marshmallow and chocolate toppings.

AND HERE'S A HOSTESS HINT! Even at the best parties, accidents happen. If a bit of ice cream slides down a fresh pinafore or Sunday suit, sponge the garment with cold or lukewarm water immediately! Phone your guest's mother, suggest she wash it as soon as possible.

74

CRANBERRY ORANGE RING
(makes 8 to 10 servings)

2 envelopes unflavored
   gelatine
½ cup cold water
1 cup fresh orange juice
4 cups whole cranberry sauce
1 tablespoon grated orange
   rind

2 tablespoons sugar
½ cup chopped walnuts
½ cup chopped celery
3 cups cottage cheese
1 or 2 tablespoons grated
   orange rind
⅓ cup chopped walnuts

Soften gelatine in cold water. Heat orange juice to boiling. Pour over gelatine. Stir until dissolved. Add cranberry sauce, 1 tablespoon of orange rind and sugar. Blend well. Chill to consistency of unbeaten egg white. Stir in ½ cup walnuts and celery. Pour into 5½-cup ring mold. Chill until firm. Combine cottage cheese, remaining orange rind, walnuts. Unmold salad on lettuce. Fill center with cottage cheese mixture. Serve as a buffet salad.

ENGLISH WALNUTS aren't really English! They acquired that name when English trading vessels were carrying them to various world ports, including American. Today over 75 percent of our supply is grown in California. But the name "English walnuts" still sticks.

BEEF AND MACARONI BAKE
(makes 6 servings)

1 pound ground chuck
½ cup chopped onion
½ cup chopped green pepper
3 tablespoons chopped pimiento
1 cup sour cream
½ teaspoon dillweed
1 teaspoon salt

⅛ teaspoon pepper
1¼ cups cream of
   mushroom soup
3 cups drained cooked
   elbow macaroni
1 cup canned onion rings
Parsley

Brown meat and onion in saucepan. Drain well. Add remaining ingredients except onion rings and parsley. Mix well. Spoon into 2-quart casserole. Bake in moderate oven (350° F.) 30 minutes. Place onion rings around casserole edge. Bake additional 10 minutes. Garnish with parsley and serve.

 END OF THE HOLIDAY HINT FOR MOTHER. To soften the "back to school" blow (while you sigh with relief now that summer's over) take the children to the beach or pool one more time. Then serve one of these party desserts.

CAKE AND COOKIE SCHOOLHOUSE, for 12 hungry school-goers. Place 2 pint bricks of vanilla ice cream end to end on rectangular tray or platter. *That's* the classroom. Take 2 pint bricks of chocolate ice cream and remove one slice from each to make them square. Cut each pint in half diagonally. Place these on top of schoolhouse to make roof. Freeze. When ice cream is firm, lay alternating colors of sugar wafers on top of "roof." Use small wafer pieces for windows, larger one for door, and one on top for the chimney. Store in the freezer until serving time.

MILE-HIGH BANANA SPLITS
(makes 6 servings)

1⅓ cups mandarin orange sections	¾ cup fresh or frozen defrosted blueberries
Syrup plus water to make ¾ cup liquid	1 tablespoon butter
4 teaspoons cornstarch	1 quart peach ice cream
⅔ cup sugar	2 bananas
1 teaspoon grated lemon rind	Sweetened whipped cream
	Slivered almonds

Drain oranges and save syrup. Chill orange sections. Add water to orange syrup to make ¾ cup. Combine cornstarch, sugar and lemon rind in saucepan. Add syrup mixture to blueberries. Mix well. Cook over medium heat until thickened and clear, stirring constantly. Remove from heat. Stir in butter. Chill. At serving time, alternate layers of ice cream, blueberry sauce and orange sections in tall parfait glasses. Slice bananas in half both lengthwise and crosswise. Place 2 or 3 banana sections vertically in top of each glass. Top with whipped cream and slivered almonds.

Parties, picnics and patios

"Have a nice weekend." Friday farewell from a sweetly smiling young lady behind the check-out counter. Struggling from the supermarket, you mentally grumble. For many, the week's hustle, bustle and scurry is almost over. Yours is about to begin.

Already your ears ache at the thought of football, basketball, boating, bowling sounds coming from the TV. Temples throb to records reverberating. You know neighborhood boys will rush through the back door; no question of where they are in "Home Sweet Home." The plaster trembles under their light, airy steps.

Admit it. There are times during the week when the *stillness* is almost deafening. The clock ticks louder than a screaming siren, and you do exaggerate. Weekends aren't schedule time. No need to race that clock. Take time to party, picnic and patio . . . without blowing the budget. Dress up old-fashioneds—noodles, corn and peaches—as Noodles Cheddar, Kernel Corn Bake, Peaches and Cheese Salad. Serve up specials—Aperitivos de Fiesta or Luau Pie. Fancy up fruit, ice cream, sherbet or cake with Tops in Toppings.

POTATO AND HAM PICNIC SALAD
(makes 8 to 10 servings)

5 cups diced cooked potatoes
½ cup sliced green onions
1 cup thinly sliced celery
1 cup shredded Cheddar cheese
2 cups diced leftover cooked ham

⅓ cup sweet pickle relish
½ teaspoon salt
½ teaspoon pepper
½ teaspoon garlic salt
1½ cups sour cream

Combine all ingredients in large bowl. Mix lightly. Chill 2 to 3 hours. Serve with fresh fruit, a bowl of relishes, toasted buns and cold, frosty glasses of homogenized milk.

Tops in toppings

STRAWBERRY BANANA TOPPING. For 2 cups, combine 1 cup mashed banana and 1 cup strawberry yogurt. Chill. Serve over chilled fresh or well-drained canned fruit on lettuce. Top with a dash of nutmeg.

BERRY GOOD BERRY SAUCE. For 1 cup sauce, combine 1 8-ounce carton boysenberry yogurt, ⅓ cup sour cream and 2 tablespoons boysenberry preserve. Chill. Serve over ice cream or sponge cake. Top with additional preserve, nuts or whipped cream.

FANCIER FRUIT. Fancy up fruit this way. For 1 cup of fruit topping, combine 1 8-ounce carton vanilla yogurt, 2 tablespoons confectioners sugar, ⅛ teaspoon nutmeg, 1 teaspoon vanilla, 1½ teaspoons grated orange peel and 2 tablespoons coconut. Mix well; chill thoroughly. Use as drained, chilled fresh or canned fruit topping.

APERITIVOS DE FIESTA
(makes 36 delicious appetizers)

1 cup (½ pint) cottage cheese	1 teaspoon poppy seeds
¼ cup deviled ham	½ teaspoon paprika
2 tablespoons finely chopped celery	¼ teaspoon pepper
	Few grains cayenne pepper
2 tablespoons finely chopped onion	6 toasted corn tortillas

Combine cottage cheese, ham, celery, onion, poppy seeds, paprika, pepper and cayenne. Mix well. Chill until ready to serve. Before serving, spread heaping tablespoon of mixture on each corn tortilla. Bake in very hot oven (475° F.) 2 to 3 minutes or until cottage cheese just begins to melt. Use very sharp knife or kitchen shears to cut each tortilla into 6 wedges. Serve at once.

CRANBERRY ROUNDS. For 8 servings, dissolve 2 3-ounce packages raspberry-flavored gelatin in 1½ cups hot water. Chill to consistency of unbeaten egg white. Stir in 1 cup whole cranberry sauce, 1 cup (8-ounce carton) red raspberry yogurt, ¼ cup chopped nuts, ¾ cup chopped celery and ⅓ cup mayonnaise. Mix well. Spoon into eight ½-cup individual molds. Chill until firm. Serve in lettuce cups.

PEACHY RASPBERRY MELBA MERINGUE
(makes 8 servings)

1 or 2 quarts Peachy Smooth Carnation ice cream	½ cup drained sliced fresh, frozen or canned peaches
9-inch baked meringue shell	Raspberry Melba Sauce

Arrange scoops of peach ice cream in meringue shell. Top with drained sliced peaches. (Defrost frozen peaches before using.) Spoon about half of warm Raspberry Sauce (see recipe below) over top. Serve sliced meringue with additional warm sauce.

RASPBERRY MELBA SAUCE. Combine 2 10-ounce packages thawed frozen raspberries, 6 tablespoons sugar and 2 tablespoons cornstarch in saucepan. Cook over medium heat until thickened and clear. Cool slightly before serving.

KERNEL CORN BAKE. For 6 to 8 servings, simmer 3½ cups (2 12-ounce cans) whole kernel corn, ¼ cup finely chopped onion and ¼ cup chopped green pepper 5 minutes in small amount of corn liquid or water. Drain. Add ½ teaspoon salt, ⅛ teaspoon pepper, 1 cup (½ pint) sour cream, 1 cup Cheddar cheese and 1 beaten egg. Mix well. Pour into buttered baking dish, 6 x 10 x 2 inches. Sprinkle with 1 cup crushed cracker crumbs. Bake in hot oven (400° F.) 10 minutes. Serve with leftover roast, hot dogs or hamburgers.

> NO ONION OR GREEN PEPPER IN THE REFRIGERATOR? Check the spice and herb shelf. Use the dehydrated green onion and green pepper there!

PEACHES AND CHEESE SALAD
(makes 6 servings)

2 cups cottage cheese
3 tablespoons sugar
½ teaspoon nutmeg
½ teaspoon cinnamon
2 tablespoons toasted sesame seeds

6 well-drained peach halves
Lettuce, watercress and
  maraschino cherries

Combine cottage cheese, sugar, nutmeg, cinnamon and sesame seeds. Mix well; chill. Place each peach half on lettuce. Spoon cottage cheese mixture on each peach half. Garnish with watercress and maraschino cherry, if desired.

SPECIAL SPINACH. For 6 to 8 servings, sauté ¼ pound sliced fresh mushrooms and ¼ cup finely chopped onion in ¼ cup melted butter or margarine. Add 1 tablespoon flour and ¼ teaspoon salt. Stir. Blend in 1 cup sour cream and 2 cups (2 10-ounce packages) drained cooked frozen chopped spinach. Heat to serving temperature, stirring.

BEAN BURGER TURNOVERS
(makes 4 to 6 servings)

1½ pounds ground chuck
2 teaspoons seasoned salt
½ cup sour cream
¼ cup fine dry bread
crumbs
Mustard
¼ cup finely chopped
green pepper

¼ cup finely chopped onion
½ cup drained mashed pork
and beans
4 slices process American
cheese

Combine chuck, seasoned salt, sour cream and crumbs. Mix gently but thoroughly. Shape mixture into 8 patties, 5 inches in diameter. Spread each patty lightly with mustard. Combine green pepper, onion and beans; mix well. Place 1 heaping tablespoon bean mixture on each patty. Fold patties in half. Seal edges well. Broil 4 inches from heat 4 to 6 minutes on each side or to desired doneness. Remove from broiler. Cut cheese slices in half to make triangles. Top each turnover with cheese triangle. Return to broiler until cheese begins to melt.

NOODLES CHEDDAR
(makes 6 to 8 servings)

1 cup cottage cheese
1½ cups sour cream
1 crushed garlic clove
1 teaspoon Worcestershire
  sauce
2 tablespoons grated onion

½ teaspoon salt
5 cups (8 ounces uncooked) hot
  cooked, drained egg noodles
1 cup shredded Cheddar
  cheese

Mix all ingredients *except* ¼ cup shredded Cheddar in bowl. Place in buttered 2-quart casserole. Sprinkle remaining Cheddar on top. Bake in hot oven (400° F.) 25 to 30 minutes or until heated through. Serve with meats barbecued on the outdoor grill.

EASIER WEEKEND COOKING. Prepare Noodles Cheddar early in the day. Spoon into buttered 2-quart casserole about an hour before dinner. Bake in hot oven (400° F.) 40 to 50 minutes.

LAST-MINUTE TUNA AND MACARONI
(makes 4 to 6 servings)

½ cup chopped onion
1 small clove crushed garlic
¼ cup chopped green pepper
2 tablespoons melted butter
1 tablespoon flour
¼ teaspoon salt
⅛ teaspoon oregano
1 teaspoon Worcestershire
  sauce

1 cup plain yogurt
1 cup processed cheese spread
1 cup (6½ or 7-ounce can)
  drained flaked tuna
½ cup drained sliced ripe
  olives
4 cups hot drained cooked
  macaroni

Sauté onion, garlic and green pepper about 3 minutes in butter. Add flour, salt, oregano and Worcestershire. Stir until blended. Add yogurt. Stir over medium heat until thickened. Add remaining ingredients. Heat to serving temperature. Stir frenquently and it's ready to serve!

TIME-SAVER. While preparing tuna mixture, have macaroni cooking according to label directions. Mix, heat, and serve with fruit or crisp vegetables for a quick but hearty meal.

LUAU PIE
(makes 9-inch pie)

8½-ounce can crushed
  pineapple
Syrup plus water to make
  1 cup
3-ounce package lemon gelatine
8 ounces softened cream
  cheese

⅔ cup mashed ripe avocado
¼ cup sugar
½ pint sour cream
9-inch baked single crust
  pie shell

Drain pineapple; reserve syrup. Add water to syrup to make 1 cup. Mix with gelatine in saucepan. Stir over medium heat until gelatine dissolves (about 5 minutes). Cool to room temperature. Beat cream cheese and avocado until smooth. Blend in sugar and sour cream. Gradually add ⅔ cup cooled gelatine; beat until well mixed. Pour into baked pie shell. Chill. Combine remaining gelatine and crushed pineapple. Spoon over avocado mixture. Chill until firm.

PRETTY PLACE MATS. Turn summer vacation treasures into patio décor. Remember the box of seashells which simply had to be packed into an already overpacked car? Use them for the patio. Wash shells in cold water, rinse and allow to dry. Coat inside and out with colorless nail polish. Glue 8 or 9 assorted-sized shells into upper left-hand corner of woven hemp place mat. (Your son probably has *numerous* leftover partly used tubes of glue in his hobby kit.) Allow shells to dry. Add "jewels" of the household—leftover beads, glitter or sparkly stones from the one-earring collection!

OCTOBER PARFAITS. For 4 parfaits, combine ½ cup chocolate ice cream topping, ½ cup marshmallow crème and ⅓ cup chopped nuts. Mix well. Using 1 or 2 pints orange sherbet, alternate with topping mix in 4 8-ounce parfait glasses. Place in freezer until serving time. Garnish with sweetened whipped cream and corn candies.

Quicker quickies

The old saying goes, "A man must work from sun to sun, but a woman's work is *never* done."

That's the way things go on days when you are a school bus substitute, due to visit the dentist, off to return those long-lost library books and attend a P.T.A. meeting. Not enough hours in the day, you say? Solve part of the problem with quicker quickies. If you have kept that emergency shelf stocked for family as well as guest meals, there's bound to be a solution.

Brighten up packaged Macaroni and Cheese mix with a Decorator Tomato Trick touch, or serve Franks and Cheese in Mugs around the fire. If it's leftover roast night, top off ice cream with 1-2-3 Fudge Sauce. Don't forget to use your prettiest mats and bright napkins to disguise your kitchen shortcuts!

MEAT LOAF IN MINUTES
(makes 4 servings)

½ cup *undiluted* Velvetized evaporated milk
1 pound ground beef
½ cup fine dry bread crumbs
1 tablespoon prepared mustard
2 tablespoons chopped onion
2 tablespoons chopped green pepper
¾ teaspoon salt
⅛ teaspoon pepper

Combine ingredients in large bowl. Mix lightly. Place in small meat loaf pan (7⅜ x 3⅝ x 2¼ inches). Bake in moderate oven (375° F.) 40 minutes. Allow to stand about 10 minutes before serving. If you *think* you're going to have a dinner crisis, make the meat loaf ahead and use it for sandwiches.

OPEN-FACE MEAT LOAF SANDWICHES. Slice meat loaf. Garnish with strip of cheese, stuffed green olives, tomato slices or dill pickles. Serve with a mug of Cool Asparagus Soup.

COOL ASPARAGUS SOUP
(makes about 3½ cups)

2 cups half and half

2 cups cooked drained
  asparagus spears

¼ teaspoon salt

Few grains pepper

1 teaspoon seasoned salt

1 tablespoon grated onion

½ teaspoon sugar

2 teaspoons lemon juice

Chopped parsley

Place all ingredients in blender. Cover and blend about 1 minute at high speed. Chill thoroughly. Serve in chilled mugs, garnished with finely chopped parsley or chives.

SAVE FURNITURE SCRATCHES. Glue felt to the bottom of ashtrays, flower bowls or candleholders to save water marks or scratches on tables.

DECORATOR TOMATO TRICK. Garnish macaroni and cheese baked from a mix or cooked hot buttered rice, with well-drained whole pear shaped tomatoes.

86

1-2-3 FUDGE SAUCE
(makes 2½ cups sauce)

1 large can *undiluted*
 Velvetized evaporated milk
2 cups sugar

3 squares unsweetened
 chocolate
1 teaspoon vanilla

Mix evaporated milk, sugar and chocolate in saucepan. Bring to boil over medium heat. Cook 5 minutes, stirring vigorously. Remove from heat. Add vanilla. Beat with rotary beater 1 minute. Serve hot or cold. (If the sauce seems a bit too thick, just add *undiluted* evaporated milk and blend before using.)

QUICK ICE CREAM CAKE. Fit a layer of plain cake into the bottom of a refrigerator tray. (Use your own leftover cake, "store bought" cake or cake from a mix.) Spread cake with ice cream. Cover ice cream with a second layer of cake. Press cake layer down lightly. Cover with foil. Keep in freezer compartment until serving time. Slice with sharp knife. Top with 1-2-3 Fudge Sauce.

BANANAS A LA MODE. Split bananas lengthwise. Place on salad or dessert dishes. Top with ice cream and 1-2-3 Fudge Sauce.

SUDDEN PUDDING. For 4 to 6 servings, pour 1 cup cold milk and 1 cup sour cream into deep mixing bowl. Add 1 package instant pudding mix. Beat with rotary beater or mixer until pudding is smooth. Turn into serving dishes and chill until firm. (This takes about 10 minutes.) Top with fruit, and dessert is ready!

PORK CHOP DINNER FOR 6

6 (½-inch thick) pork chops
1 tablespoon butter
½ cup thinly sliced green
   onions
2 cups sliced potatoes

2 cups sliced carrots
1¼ cups (10¾-ounce can)
   cream of mushroom soup
1 cup *undiluted* Carnation
   Evaporated Milk

Brown chops thoroughly in butter. Drain off excess fat. Add green onions, potatoes and carrots. Mix mushroom soup and Carnation; pour over all ingredients. Cover and simmer 30 to 40 minutes or until chops and vegetables are tender. Stir occasionally. Serve as a complete dinner.

QUICK HAMBURGER TRICK. Prepare your favorite recipe for hamburgers, using 1½ pounds ground chuck. Form 6 patties. Brown burgers in small amount of oil or margarine. Pour off fat. Add one can of Sweet 'n Sour Cookbook Sauce. Cover and simmer 15 minutes. Then serve 6.

QUICK HOT DOG TRICK. Combine 1 8-ounce can tomato sauce with ¼ cup sweet pickle relish and 1 teaspoon prepared mustard in saucepan. Heat 5 minutes. Hot or cold, it's a new flavor touch for grilled hot dogs.

JIFFY STEW AND DUMPLINGS
(makes 6 to 8 servings)

2 cups sifted flour
1 teaspoon salt
4 teaspoons baking powder
½ teaspoon nutmeg
¼ teaspoon pepper
1 well-beaten egg

3 tablespoons oil
½ cup *undiluted* Velvetized
   evaporated milk
½ cup water
2 cans (2 to 2½ pounds each)
   beef stew, heated

Sift dry ingredients together. Add egg, oil, evaporated milk and water. Mix well. Drop by teaspoons onto hot canned beef stew. Be sure to drop dumplings on meat cubes. Cover. Simmer 25 minutes. Serve at once.

OVEN-EASY CHILI-BEEF BAKE
(makes 6 servings)

1 pound ground chuck	1 tablespoon chili powder
⅔ cup *undiluted* Velvetized evaporated milk	1 tablespoon flour
	1 cup tomato sauce
½ cup chopped onion	1½ cups drained chili beans
½ cup chopped green pepper	½ cup drained sliced ripe olives
1 teaspoon salt	
¼ teaspoon seasoned pepper	2 cups corn chips

Combine chuck, evaporated milk, onion, green pepper, salt, seasoned pepper and chili powder in large skillet. Cook over medium heat until browned, stirring occasionally. Add flour, stir well. Add tomato sauce, chili beans and olives. Blend well. Cover bottom of 1½-quart casserole with 1 cup corn chips. Pour in meat mixture. Top with remaining corn chips. Bake in moderate oven (350° F.) 30 minutes.

> THERE'S TIME FOR YOUR BEAUTY BREAK if you prepare casserole mixture early in the day, then let your older daughter or baby-sitter assemble it before baking.

FRANKS AND CHEESE IN MUGS
(makes 6 to 8 servings)

4 frankfurters
1 medium chopped onion
1 tablespoon butter
2 tablespoons flour
1 teaspoon salt
¼ teaspoon pepper
10½-ounce can chicken
    broth

2½ cups cream-style
    corn
¼ cup chopped parsley
2 cups milk
1 cup grated sharp
    Cheddar cheese

Slice frankfurters in thin circles. Sauté onion in butter in large saucepan. Stir in flour and seasonings. Add broth, corn, parsley and frankfurters. Stir in milk. Heat to serving temperature but *do not boil*. Add Cheddar, stir and serve at once in warm mugs.

FIRST AID FOR RECORDINGS. Don't treat records as if they were paper plates. Instead of leaving them on the player, place them gently back in their plastic covers and outer jackets. Stack them vertically in a record holder to prevent warping.

RICH AND SAUCY BEANS
(makes 2 quarts)

1 cup chopped onion
½ cup chopped green pepper
2 tablespoons margarine
⅔ cup tomato paste
½ cup deviled ham

2 tablespoons prepared
    mustard
¼ cup brown sugar
7½ to 8 cups pork and
    beans

Sauté onion and green pepper in margarine. Add tomato paste, deviled ham, mustard and brown sugar. Mix well. Stir beans gently into other ingredients. Simmer 15 minutes, stirring occasionally to prevent sticking. Delicious with leftover sliced ham, frankfurters or hamburgers.

MAKES-A-MEAL SALAD

(serves 8 or 10—enough for the family and for leftovers, too)

¼ cup lemon juice
1 cup *undiluted* Velvetized
 evaporated milk
¼ cup salad dressing
1 teaspoon salt
⅛ teaspoon pepper
¼ teaspoon crushed dillweed
⅛ teaspoon celery seed
2 tablespoons pickle relish
3 cups cooked drained salad
 macaroni

1 cup sliced celery
¾ cup chopped onion
1 cup well-drained peas and
 carrots
12-ounce can diced luncheon
 meat
2 tablespoons chopped
 pimiento

Stir lemon juice into evaporated milk until milk thickens. Add salad dressing, salt, pepper, dill, celery seed and relish. Combine remaining ingredients in large bowl. Pour dressing over macaroni mixture and toss lightly until blended. Chill about 2 hours. Serve on lettuce cups, garnished with carrot curls.

MAYBE YOU DIDN'T KNOW SANDWICHES ARE LORDLY FOOD. They were named for John Montagu, 4th Earl of Sandwich, back in the middle of the 18th century. But you *do* know Refrigerator Raiders eat lots of them.

DEVILED HAM AND CHEESEWICHES. For 8 sandwiches, combine ⅓ cup deviled ham, 1 cup cottage cheese, 1 tablespoon minced onion, 2 tablespoons sweet pickle relish and 3 tablespoons sour cream. Blend well and spread on whole wheat or dark rye bread for hungry ones.

HELP-YOURSELF TRAY. Arrange cold sliced meat loaf, cheese and cold cuts on salad tray. Put buttered bread slices in plastic sandwich bag, and relish dish of celery cuts, dill pickle slices and chilled olives beside it.

TEEN BURGERS WITH MUSTARD SAUCE
(makes 4 juicy burgers)

1 tablespoon margarine	2 tablespoons prepared
1 tablespoon flour	mustard
½ teaspoon salt	¼ cup sliced stuffed olives
1 cup *undiluted* Velvetized	2 tablespoons chopped parsley
evaporated milk	

Melt margarine in saucepan over low heat. Add flour and salt. Slowly stir in evaporated milk. Cook over medium heat until sauce thickens (about 5 minutes). Add mustard, olives and parsley. Serve sauce over burgers.

FOR BURGERS. Mix 1 pound ground chuck, ½ cup cracker crumbs and ½ cup *undiluted* Velvetized evaporated milk. Salt and pepper to taste. Mix all ingredients lightly but thoroughly. Broil or pan fry to desired doneness.

KABOBS POLYNESIAN. Place chilled chunks of pineapple, strawberries, slices of banana, whole seedless grapes and maraschino cherries on toothpicks or small skewers. Arrange kabobs on platter around a bowl of chilled sour cream.

SPEEDY SHERBET PUNCH
(for 14 thirsty golfers or baseball-ers)

1 cup chilled tea	2 cups chilled ginger ale
1 cup orange juice	1 or 2 pints pineapple or
2 cups pineapple juice	orange sherbet

Combine tea, orange juice and pineapple juice. Chill. When the thirsty ones arrive, add ginger ale. Place in punch cups and top with a spoon or scoop of sherbet.

AFTER-THE-GAME SLOPPY JOES
(makes about 6 servings)

1½ pounds ground beef	1⅔ cups *undiluted*
½ cup chopped onion	Velvetized evaporated milk
¼ teaspoon garlic salt	1 cup chili sauce
2 tablespoons flour	6 toasted hamburger buns

Brown beef and onion in frying pan over medium heat 5 minutes. Drain off fat. Stir in garlic salt and flour until blended. Gradually add evaporated milk. Stir over low heat constantly until thickened. Add chili sauce slowly. Heat to serving temperature. Serve over buns.

HOT DOG CHILIBURGER SAUCE. For 6 cups sauce, sauté 1 cup onion in 2 tablespoons oil. Stir in ⅔ cup tomato paste, 1 cup water, 2 teaspoons chili powder, 1 teaspoon salt, 1 teaspoon sugar and 3¾ cups drained canned chili beans. Simmer, uncovered, 20 minutes. Stir often to prevent sticking. Serve over grilled frankfurters on toasted buns. (Or it's equally good over hamburgers or grilled cube steaks!)

TAKE-ALONG CHOWDER
(makes 6 cups chowder)

½ cup chopped onion	⅔ cup water
⅓ cup chopped green pepper	2 cups canned pork and beans
3 tablespoons margarine	1 cup tomato sauce
2 tablespoons flour	1½ teaspoons seasoned salt
1⅔ cups *undiluted*	3 coarsely chopped wieners
Velvetized evaporated milk	

Sauté onion and green pepper in margarine until tender in medium saucepan. Stir in flour. Slowly add evaporated milk, stirring constantly. Add remaining ingredients. Stir over medium heat about 20 minutes. Place in wide-mouth vacuum jar.

Unhurried eating

There comes a time to get off that 5:45 P.M. week-night dinner indigestion express!

Weekends are the time for no scramble, no scurry and a few moments of adult-type peace and quiet. Whether it's just you two or a crew, take time to breathe a bit and call time your own.

Maybe it's something simple as a slice of Spicy Raisin Cream Pie and coffee after the children are in bed. Maybe it's a Block Party where everyone pools kitchen talents! If you are serving, make it Supper on a Skewer. If you're going, a Take-It-To-The-Party Asparagus Salad or a casserole of Rice California is delicious and welcome.

BE A GOOD-AND-EASY BRUNCH HOSTESS. Serve Sausage and Eggs. Less last-minute fuss. Summertime, serve them with melon and lime slices. Wintertime, orange or grapefruit slices.

SAUSAGE AND EGGS
(makes 4 servings)

4 English muffin halves	1 tablespoon cornstarch
4 poached or scrambled eggs	14½-ounce can Contadina
8 hot cooked link sausages	Stewed Tomatoes

Toast muffin halves. Place eggs and sausages on muffin halves. Mix cornstarch and tomatoes. Cook until thick. Spoon over muffins.

SPICY RAISIN CREAM PIE
(makes 9-inch pie)

1 3½-ounce package lemon
  pudding and pie filling mix
¾ cup sugar
¼ teaspoon cinnamon
⅛ teaspoon nutmeg
1½ cups water
2 beaten eggs

1 cup seedless raisins
1 cup sour cream
9-inch baked pie shell
2 tablespoons confectioners
  sugar
1 cup all-purpose cream

Combine pudding mix, sugar, cinnamon, nutmeg and ¼ *cup* water in saucepan. Blend in eggs and raisins. Stir in *remaining* 1¼ cups water. Cook over medium heat until mixture comes to full boil, stirring constantly. Cool 5 minutes. Add sour cream and blend well. Pour into baked pie shell. Chill 1 to 2 hours. Add confectioners sugar to cream. Whip until soft peaks form. Spoon on top of pie and serve.

TAKE-IT-TO-THE-PARTY ASPARAGUS SALAD
(makes 6 servings)

2 tablespoons (2 envelopes)
  unflavored gelatine
½ cup cold water
10½-ounce can cream of
  asparagus soup
1 teaspoon seasoned salt
⅛ teaspoon pepper
1 teaspoon lemon juice

2 drops hot pepper sauce
1 cup cottage cheese
1 cup sour cream
2 teaspoons grated onion
1 tablespoon chopped pimiento
½ cup chopped celery
1 14½-ounce can drained
  whole green asparagus spears

Soften gelatine in water. Combine gelatine, soup, salt, pepper, lemon juice and hot pepper sauce in saucepan. Heat, stirring constantly to dissolve gelatine. Beat cottage cheese until smooth. Add sour cream; blend well. Stir in soup mixture, onion, pimiento and celery. Chill until mixture mounds when dropped from spoon. Cut asparagus into ½-inch pieces. Fold into gelatine mixture. Chill in 5-cup mold.

CHERRY CREAM FROSTING. Cream ½ cup butter or margarine until light and fluffy. Add 4¾ cups (1 pound) sifted confectioners sugar, 1 tablespoon maraschino cherry juice and ¼ cup sour cream. Beat until smooth and fluffy. Add additional sour cream, 1 teaspoon at a time, until of desired spreading consistency. Use to frost 2 cooled 9-inch cake layers. Garnish with well-drained maraschino cherry halves and chopped nuts.

EASY-ON-THE-BUDGET BARBECUED FRANKS AND LIMAS
(makes 6 servings)

1 pound dry baby lima beans	2 teaspoons dry mustard
6 cups water	1 tablespoon vinegar
2 teaspoons salt	⅓ cup molasses
10 frankfurters	2 cups tomato sauce
½ cup chopped onion	½ teaspoon salt

Wash beans. Place in 4-quart saucepan. Add water and salt. Cover and bring to boil. Boil 2 minutes. Remove from heat. Allow beans to soak 1 hour. *Do not* remove cover or change water. Bring beans to boil. Reduce heat and simmer until beans are tender, 45 to 60 minutes. Drain. Cut 4 frankfurters into crosswise slices. Make diagonal slits in remaining 6 franks. Combine sliced frankfurters, beans and remaining ingredients. Pour into 2-quart casserole or baking dish (12 x 7½ x 2 inches). Arrange remaining 6 franks on top. Bake in moderate oven (350° F.) 30 to 40 minutes. Serve with toasted buns and relishes.

SUPPER ON A SKEWER
(makes 6 to 8 servings)

⅔ cup tomato paste
¼ cup oil
½ cup water
½ cup minced onion
1 teaspoon salt
⅛ teaspoon pepper
1 crushed clove garlic
1 tablespoon Worcestershire
sauce

3 pounds (1 inch thick)
sirloin tip steak
16 to 24 small boiling onions
2 green peppers
16 to 24 mushroom crowns
¼ cup butter
16 to 24 cherry tomatoes

Combine tomato paste, oil, water, onion, salt, pepper, garlic and
Worcestershire in saucepan. Mix well. Simmer, uncovered, 10
minutes. Cut steak into 1½-inch squares. Combine hot marinade
and steak in large bowl. Mix well. Cover. Refrigerate several hours
or overnight. Clean onions. Cut green peppers into 2-inch pieces.
Parboil onions and green peppers 2 minutes. Drain. Sauté mushrooms in butter. Save butter. Alternate steak, onion, green pepper,
mushrooms and tomatoes on 6 or 8 12-inch skewers. Place on
broiler pans. Brush meat with remaining marinade. Brush vegetables with butter. Broil 4 to 5 inches from heat, turning often
and basting with butter, 15 to 20 minutes. Serve at once.

UPSIDE-DOWN PEACH BAVARIAN
(makes 8 to 10 servings)

1 14 or 14½-ounce package
gingerbread mix
½ gallon peach ice cream
¼ cup brown sugar
¼ teaspoon cinnamon

⅓ cup chopped pecans
2 peeled sliced fresh peaches or
1-pound can drained sliced
peaches
Maraschino cherry halves

Prepare gingerbread according to package directions. Place in buttered wax-paper-lined 9-inch round cake pan. Bake in moderate oven (350° F.) 30 to 35 minutes. Cool. Remove from pan. Line 9-inch round cake pan with aluminum foil, allowing 2-inch overlap around edges. Press ice cream into pan. Freeze at least 2 hours or until serving time. Combine brown sugar, cinnamon and pecans. Mix well. To serve, place gingerbread topside-down on large platter. Place ice cream on top of cake. Remove foil. Sprinkle top of ice cream with brown sugar mixture. Top with peach slices and cherry halves.

RICE CALIFORNIA
(makes 6 servings)

8 slices bacon
½ cup chopped onion
½ cup chopped green pepper
½ cup drained sliced
mushrooms
3½ cups tomato sauce

1 teaspoon chili powder
½ teaspoon salt
⅛ teaspoon pepper
3 cups hot cooked white rice
½ cup shredded process
American cheese

Fry bacon until crisp in large skillet. Drain and break into small pieces. Remove all but 2 tablespoons bacon fat. Sauté onion and green pepper in fat. Add mushrooms, tomato sauce, chili powder, salt and pepper. Simmer, uncovered, 15 minutes. Stir into rice. Simmer, uncovered, additional 15 minutes. Stir occasionally to prevent sticking. Top with cheese and serve with steaks, roast beef or baked ham.

CHEESE AND SEAFOOD RING
(makes 6 to 8 servings)

1 tablespoon (1 envelope) unflavored gelatine
1 cup milk
2 cups cottage cheese
2 ounces blue cheese
1 teaspoon seasoned salt
¼ teaspoon salt
1 teaspoon Worcestershire sauce
1 tablespoon grated onion
¼ cup finely chopped green pepper
1 tablespoon chopped pimiento
3 cups cooked shell macaroni
Chilled fresh or canned crab, shrimp or lobster

Soften gelatine in *½ cup* milk. Heat, stirring constantly to dissolve gelatine. Combine cottage cheese and blue cheese. Beat until smooth. Add remaining milk, gelatine mixture, seasoned salt, salt, Worcestershire, onion, green pepper and pimiento. Blend thoroughly. Add macaroni. Mix well. Spoon into 5½-cup ring mold. Chill until set. Unmold and fill center of ring with seafood. Garnish with tomatoes, and serve with hot rolls for buffet luncheon or dinner guests.

GAZPACHO
(makes 5⅓ cups)

1 minced clove garlic
1⅔ cups round peeled tomatoes
2 cups peeled chopped cucumber
½ cup finely chopped green pepper
½ cup finely chopped onion
2 cups tomato juice
2 tablespoons oil
3 tablespoons vinegar
½ teaspoon salt
⅛ teaspoon pepper
⅛ teaspoon red pepper sauce

Place garlic, tomatoes, cucumber, green pepper and onion in blender. Cover. Blend until mixture is almost smooth. Pour into pitcher. Stir in remaining ingredients. Chill. Serve in individual chilled bowls or mugs over ice cubes.

HOW TO SERVE GAZPACHO? Place separate dishes of chopped peeled tomatoes, chopped green pepper, chopped cucumber and croutons on tray with soup. Let each guest "season" his own.

101

AVOCADO MADRILENE
(makes 6 servings)

1⅔ cups tomato puree
2 envelopes unflavored
gelatine
½ cup cold water
1¼ cups canned beef
consommé

1½ cups water
¼ teaspoon salt
3 avocados
Salt
Pepper
Lemon slices

Simmer tomato puree in large saucepan until it is reduced to about ¾ cup. Stir occasionally. Soften gelatine in ½ *cup* water. Add consommé, 1½ cups water, salt and softened gelatine to puree. Heat to boiling, stirring occasionally. Pour into 8-inch-square pan. Chill until set (about 3 hours). Cut into small cubes. Just before serving, halve, peel, and seed avocados. Place avocado halves on lettuce. Sprinkle each half with salt and pepper. Mound avocado halves with cubed madrilène. Garnish with lemon slices and serve at once.

MINESTRONE ROMA
(makes 6 to 8 servings)

2½ cups condensed beef
consommé
4 cups water
½ cup lentils
3 diced bacon strips
⅔ cup tomato paste
1 package spaghetti sauce mix
2 cloves garlic
½ teaspoon seasoned salt

½ teaspoon seasoned pepper
½ cup coarsely shredded
cabbage
½ cup small elbow macaroni
1 10-ounce package frozen
mixed vegetables
2 tablespoons finely chopped
parsley

Pour consommé, water and lentils in large saucepan. Add bacon. Cover and simmer 1 hour. Add tomato paste and spaghetti sauce mix. Mix well. Insert toothpick into each garlic clove. Add garlic, seasoned salt, seasoned pepper and cabbage. Cover and simmer additional 25 minutes. Remove garlic. Bring soup to boil. Add macaroni, vegetables and parsley. Simmer until macaroni and vegetables are tender.

MEXICAN SOUP STEW
(makes 10 to 12 cups)

1⅓ cups dry red or
  garbanzo beans
2½ pounds beef short ribs
1 quart water
1⅔ cups round peeled
  tomatoes
1½ cups finely chopped onion
2 cloves crushed garlic

1 cup finely chopped celery
½ teaspoon pepper
4 teaspoons salt
2 teaspoons chili powder
½ cup water
½ cup *undiluted* Velvetized
  evaporated milk

Wash beans. Cover with water and soak overnight. Drain. Brown
short ribs in large saucepan. Pour off fat. Add beans and 1 quart
water. Cover. Simmer 2 hours. Add more water as needed to keep
meat and beans well covered. Remove ribs. Cut meat from bone.
Discard bones and fat; place meat into soup. Add remaining ingredients except evaporated milk. Cook 1 hour. Just before serving,
add evaporated milk. Serve with warm, crusty sourdough or garlic
bread slices.

SWISS CHEESE ISN'T ALL FROM SWITZER-
LAND. Much of our tasty "Swiss" is made right
in Wisconsin, U.S.A., the heart of our dairying
industry!

MONTREAL FAVORITE QUICHE LORRAINE
(makes 5 to 6 servings)

10 slices fried bacon
9-inch unbaked pie shell
3 ounces sliced Swiss cheese
1 tablespoon flour
¼ teaspoon salt

⅛ teaspoon black pepper
1⅔ cups *undiluted* Velvetized
  evaporated milk
4 beaten eggs
1 tablespoon grated onion

Crumble 6 fried bacon slices in unbaked pie shell. Cover with
cheese slices. Combine flour and seasonings. Gradually add evaporated milk. Add beaten eggs to milk mixture; blend well. Stir in
grated onion and pour into pie shell. Bake in hot oven (400° F.)
25 to 30 minutes or until knife inserted comes out clean. Garnish
with remaining bacon slices. Serve at once.

LOBSTER SEAFOOD SHELLS
(makes 6 servings)

1 cup fresh cooked crab,
lobster or shrimp
1 cup soft bread crumbs
¾ cup mayonnaise
1 cup sour cream
4 finely chopped hard-cooked
eggs
2 tablespoons grated onion

½ cup finely chopped celery
¼ cup sliced stuffed green
olives
¾ teaspoon salt
Few grains pepper
½ cup soft buttered bread
crumbs

Break crab, lobster or shrimp into bite-sized pieces. (Use 6½ to 7½-ounce can of crab, lobster or shrimp if fresh seafood isn't available.) Mix with all remaining ingredients *except* bread crumbs. Spoon into 1-quart casserole or 6 individual heatproof shells. Top with buttered crumbs. Bake individual servings in moderate oven (350° F.) until mixture begins to bubble (20 to 25 minutes). Bake in 1-quart casserole 25 to 30 minutes. Garnish with additional olive slices. Serve with a green or fruit salad and coffee.

HASH AND EGGS FOR BRUNCH
(makes 4 to 6 servings)

½ cup chopped onion
¼ cup chopped green pepper
3 tablespoons butter or
margarine
1¾ cups canned roast beef
hash
½ cup fine dry bread crumbs

2 tablespoons chopped
pimiento
½ teaspoon salt
2 cups cottage cheese
4 eggs
¼ cup grated Parmesan
cheese

Sauté onion and green pepper in melted butter until tender. Stir in hash, bread crumbs, pimiento and salt. Heat until mixture leaves sides of pan. Spread evenly in bottom of buttered 10 x 6 x 2-inch baking dish. Beat cottage cheese at high speed on electric mixer until smooth. Add eggs, one at a time, beating well after each addition. Beat in Parmesan. Pour over meat in baking dish. Bake in moderate oven (375° F.) 35 to 40 minutes or until top layer is golden brown and set. Garnish with chopped parsley.

VIP NIGHT MENU
No-Salad-Tonight Vegetable Dip
Chicken Barbecue on a Spit
Do-Ahead Corn Relish in Tomato Cups
Buttered Carrots
Hot Rolls with Butter
Watermelon Waikiki

Things you can do ahead

PREPARE Vegetable Dip from the recipe on page 18. Store in refrigerator in covered clean glass jar or serving dish. Dip flavors are better blended if they are prepared ahead of time.

CLEAN chicken and prepare Barbecue Sauce. That recipe is on page 8.

TRIM carrots, scrub or peel and slice into lengthwise strips. Cover with water.

PREPARE Do-Ahead Corn Relish from the recipe on page 41. You may wish to serve it in tomato cups or in an attractive bowl next to the chicken.

PREPARE Watermelon Waikiki (page 53). Cover the watermelon and, at dessert time, just top it with sherbet.

COLLECT serving and special kitchen utensils. Avoid the search for the ice cream scoop, just as you're ready to top dessert.

START the barbecue fire 45 minutes before the chicken should be barbecued. Coals take time to ignite.

AFTER guests arrive, let the children pass dips, empty ashtrays and remove beverage glasses, so that you can enjoy your own party.

When you're cooking for a crowd, you need a few short-cuts.

USE your electric or battery-operated carving knife to slice sourdough bread, English muffins, tomatoes, cucumbers or cabbage wedges for a corned beef and cabbage dinner.

KEEP a "party saver" in the freezer: Cheese Spaghetti for 12, a Do-Ahead Potato Puff or a pie shell that turns into a Montreal Favorite Quiche Lorraine.

SERVE help-yourself appetizers. Prepare a tray of shrimp, chilled green or ripe olives and any one of the dip ideas in Good-and-Easy.

KEEP Cookbook Sauces on the kitchen shelf. Italian Sauce short-cuts spaghetti topping and Lasagne. Sweet 'n Sour Sauce gives a new flavor change to ribs, pork chops or leftovers.

MAKE A BACKWARDS TIMETABLE and, the first few times you have guests, tape it to a kitchen cupboard, the refrigerator or in any handy kitchen spot. Set a timer to remind yourself of a kitchen task when you're meeting and greeting guests.

At any meal, put your best foot forward. Don't panic if an unexpected guest arrives. You may cringe at the thought of *only* having stew. To the traveler who's lived on hotel menus (and they become remarkably similar) or mentally fastens his seat belt as he sits down to your dinner table, hearty stew, tender hot buttered rolls, fruit and cheese for dessert become ambrosia!

Vegetable variety

"Eat your carrots if you want curly hair!"

This was one of the many old fables about vegetable eating that started in great-grandmother's day. She probably used it as a disguise for the vegetables-are-good-for-you story. Use it today and you'll probably be greeted with "I don't *want* curly hair!" as your daughter races for a brush to smooth her long, straight locks.

A few years ago, it wasn't possible to provide all of today's vegetable variety. Now, improved refrigeration and shipping methods as well as a whole new group of bright, interesting frozen or canned vegetable combinations provide a never-ending parade of new ways to serve them.

Turn on appetites! Limp, unseasoned, overcooked, unattractive vegetables are about as appealing as closet-cleaning-day clothes at a cocktail party. Read the lable directions on canned and frozen vegetables carefully. Add a few seasoning tricks like those coming up, and sneak a new, unfamiliar vegetable into a meal where the main dish and dessert are sure-fire family favorites.

THE TOURING TOMATO. In 4 centuries, the tomato has had many names and traveled many lands. Originally from a home high in the Andes, it has shared mysterious secrets of early Netherlands herbalists, flourished on the sunny slopes of southern Italy, bowed in famous French court circles as the "pomme d'amour" and bloomed in the stately flower garden of Thomas Jefferson. Now there's a whole group of lively tomato (and other vegetable) ideas to serve from the 8 Great Tomato Folks. Look for them on the labels of the red, white and green cans in your market.

SWEET POTATOES IN ORANGE SHELLS
(makes 6 to 8 servings)

4 oranges
3 cups (2 1-pound cans) well-
drained sweet potatoes
3 tablespoons butter
½ teaspoon cinnamon

2 tablespoons firmly packed
brown sugar
⅔ cup *undiluted* Velvetized
evaporated milk
Marshmallows, if desired

Halve oranges crosswise. Remove orange sections from each half
with grapefruit knife. Scoop out any remaining membrane. Scal-
lop shell edges, if desired. Chill shells until ready to use. Chop
oranges to make 1 cup. Mash sweet potatoes; mix with remaining
ingredients except marshmallows in saucepan. Cook over medium
heat until butter melts and mixture is hot. Drain chopped oranges;
mix with potatoes. Spoon into orange shells. Top with marshmallows.
Place on cookie sheet. Bake in hot oven (400° F.) 3 or 4 minutes or
until marshmallows are golden. Serve at once.

DO-AHEAD POTATO PUFF
(makes 6 servings)

6 medium potatoes, peeled
¾ cup half and half
1½ teaspoons salt
⅓ cup grated sharp
Cheddar cheese

¼ cup butter or margarine
1 teaspoon dry mustard
¼ cup finely chopped dry or
green onions

Cook potatoes in boiling, salted water until tender. Drain. Beat
with mixer or potato masher. Add remaining ingredients. Mix well.
Place in 1½-quart buttered casserole. Bake in moderate oven
(375° F.) 50 to 60 minutes.

DO-AHEAD HINT. Prepare puff earlier in the day.
Refrigerate, and bake for 60 minutes on busy days.

EGGPLANT PARMESAN
(makes 6 servings)

1 cup chopped onion
1 minced clove garlic
1 tablespoon salad oil
1⅔ cups round peeled
  tomatoes
1 bay leaf
½ teaspoon oregano
½ teaspoon salt

½ cup grated Parmesan
  cheese
¼ cup seasoned bread crumbs
1 pound eggplant
2 eggs
½ teaspoon salt
⅛ teaspoon pepper
½ cup oil

Sauté onion and garlic in 1 tablespoon oil. Add tomatoes, bay leaf, oregano and salt. Simmer 15 minutes. Remove bay leaf. Combine Parmesan and bread crumbs. Pare eggplant; cut into ¼-inch slices. Beat eggs with salt and pepper. Dip eggplant slices in egg. Fry in ½ cup oil until well browned. Drain on paper towels. Place layer of eggplant in 12 x 7 x 2-inch baking dish. Spoon half of sauce over eggplant. Sprinkle half of cheese mixture on top. Repeat layers. Bake in moderate oven (350° F.) 25 minutes and serve at once.

CORN is native to America. Centuries before Columbus discovered the New World, sweet corn was an important part of the life of the Indians of the Americas. There are Norse sailors' legends about it, dating back to the Icelandic sagas and Indian myths.

25-MINUTE CORN CREOLE
(makes 4 servings)

¼ cup chopped onion
2 tablespoons chopped
  green pepper
1 tablespoon butter
½ teaspoon cornstarch
¼ teaspoon salt

⅛ teaspoon pepper
1⅔ cups round peeled
  tomatoes
1½ cups drained whole
  kernel corn

Sauté onion and green pepper in butter. Stir in cornstarch, salt and pepper. Add tomatoes and corn. Simmer, stirring occasionally 20 to 25 minutes, and it's ready to serve.

GREEN BEANS FAR EAST
(makes 4 to 6 servings)

9-ounce package frozen cut green beans
⅓ cup finely chopped onion
1 tablespoon butter
½ teaspoon sugar
½ teaspoon vinegar
½ teaspoon seasoned salt
Few grains pepper
⅔ cup sour cream
⅔ cup sliced water chestnuts
Pimiento, if desired

Cook beans as label directs. Drain. Sauté onion in butter. Add sugar, vinegar, seasonings and sour cream. Heat to serving temperature. *Do not boil.* Add water chestnuts and sour cream mixture to beans. Heat and serve. Garnish with pimiento.

WORLD-FAMOUS TRAVELER . . . that's Mr. Potato! Four hundred years ago, the conquistadores escorted the potato from South America to Spain. Potato use spread to France, Germany and other parts of Europe. Mr. Potato became such an important part of Irish meals that the 1847 crop failure moved him to the United States.

FLUFFIER BAKED POTATOES
(makes 4 to 6 servings)

4 large or 6 medium baking potatoes
Shortening
6 tablespoons butter
½ cup finely chopped onion
1 tablespoon chopped parsley
1 cup sour cream
¾ teaspoon salt
⅛ teaspoon pepper
1 cup grated Cheddar cheese
Sour cream
Chopped parsley

Wash and dry potatoes. Rub lightly with shortening. Bake on cookie sheet in very hot oven (450° F.) 45 to 50 minutes or until done. Melt butter in large saucepan; remove 2 tablespoons. Sauté onion and 1 tablespoon parsley in remaining butter. Stir in 1 cup sour cream, salt and pepper. Keep over low heat. Slice off top of each potato. Scoop out potato into sour cream mixture, being careful not to break shells. Set shells aside. Whip potatoes and sour cream until fluffy. Add cheese. Spoon into shells. Brush with remaining melted butter. Bake 10 minutes in very hot oven (450° F.) or until lightly browned. Serve topped with additional sour cream and chopped parsley.

DILLY BEETS
(makes 4 to 6 servings)

4 cups canned julienne beets
2 tablespoons grated onion
¾ teaspoon sugar
½ teaspoon salt
¼ teaspoon pepper
½ teaspoon ground cumin
1 cup sour cream
½ teaspoon dillweed

Drain beets, reserving ⅔ cup liquid. Combine beets, beet liquid, onion, sugar, salt, pepper and cumin in saucepan. Bring just to boiling over medium heat, stirring occasionally. Drain off all but ¼ cup liquid. Add sour cream. Stir constantly over low heat to serving temperature. Place in warm serving bowl and sprinkle with dill.

DILL JUST FOR PICKLES? No, not at all. Dill, a relative of the parsley family, adds a new flavor touch to vegetables, soups and dressings.

AU GRATIN CAULIFLOWER
(makes 4 to 6 servings)

1 cup cottage cheese
1 tablespoon butter
1 tablespoon flour
½ cup homogenized milk
½ cup shredded process
   American cheese
1 tablespoon chopped pimiento
½ teaspoon dillweed
½ teaspoon salt
⅛ teaspoon pepper
2 10-ounce packages cooked
   drained frozen cauliflower
½ cup toasted small
   bread cubes

Beat cottage cheese until smooth. Melt butter in saucepan. Blend in flour. Add milk. Stir constantly over low heat until thickened. Add cottage cheese, American cheese, pimiento, dill, salt and pepper. Stir until American cheese melts. Place cauliflower in buttered 1-quart casserole. Pour sauce over cauliflower. Sprinkle with bread cubes. Bake in moderate oven (350° F.) about 15 minutes or until cheese sauce is bubbly and bread cubes browned. Garnish with parsley.

BROCCOLI WITH A CRUNCH
(makes 6 to 8 servings)

2 10-ounce packages frozen broccoli spears
2 cups sour cream
½ teaspoon garlic salt
1 teaspoon Worcestershire sauce
¾ cup cornflake crumbs
1 tablespoon milk

Cook broccoli according to package directions. Drain. Mix sour cream, salt and Worcestershire. Coat each spear with sour cream mixture. Cover with crumbs. Place in one layer in buttered 12 x 7½ x 2-inch baking dish. Bake in hot oven (400° F.) 20 minutes. Add milk to remaining sour cream mixture. Heat to serving temperature but *do not boil.* Serve with broccoli.

OLD-FASHIONED SCALLOPED TOMATOES. To serve 4 to 6, dice 6 slices bacon. Fry with ½ cup chopped onion in skillet. Drain off fat. Add 3½ cups round peeled tomatoes, 1 teaspoon sugar, ½ teaspoon salt and ⅛ teaspoon pepper. Stir to break tomatoes. Place half of tomato mixture in 1½-quart casserole. Top with 2 cups (about 6 slices bread) soft bread crumbs. Add remaining tomato mixture. Sprinkle ½ cup shredded process American cheese around edge of casserole. Bake in moderate oven (375° F.) 25 minutes.

GREEN BEANS MEXICALI
(makes 6 to 8 servings)

1 minced clove garlic
¼ cup chopped green pepper
1 cup onion rings
1 tablespoon oil
1⅔ cups round peeled tomatoes
¼ cup chopped green chiles
1 teaspoon salt
⅛ teaspoon pepper
⅛ teaspoon oregano leaves
2 9-ounce packages frozen whole or cut green beans

Sauté garlic, green pepper and onion rings in oil in large skillet until tender. Add tomatoes, green chiles, salt, pepper and oregano. Mix to break up tomatoes. Bring to boil. Reduce heat and simmer 15 minutes. Cook green beans according to package directions. Drain beans. Place in center of vegetable bowl. Spoon tomato mixture around edges of beans.

Measuring mistakes

When the "perfected recipe" doesn't come out perfect, it's easiest to blame home economists who can't cook or cookbook writers who can't write! But before you write that blistering complaint letter, check yourself.

1. NESTED measuring cups aren't for the birds. Rice, flour, sugar and other dry ingredients should be spooned gently into the appropriate cup. Each one has 1 cup, ½ cup, ⅓ cup and ¼ cup identified on the bottom or side. *Spoon gently.* No shake, no tap, no tamp-down dry ingredients, or you'll have an improper (and sometimes recipe-wrecking) measurement.

2. EFFICIENCY isn't always efficient. Don't sift flour right into the measuring cup. Sift it onto a piece of wax paper or foil. Spoon into the cup.

3. LEVEL dry ingredients with the straight edge of a spatula or knife. Spoon remainder into the canister or package.

4. USE liquid-measuring cups for oil, water, milk or other liquids. These are usually plastic or glass cups with a pouring spout. For less than ¼ cup of liquid or dry ingredients, it's more accurate to use measuring spoons. Confused about measurements? Try this . . .

THIS IS THE SAME AS	THIS
3 teaspoons	1 tablespoon
4 tablespoons	¼ cup
8 tablespoons	½ cup
16 tablespoons	1 cup
2 cups	1 pint
2 pints or 4 cups	1 quart
1 stick (¼ pound) butter or margarine)	8 tablespoons or ½ cup

Baking a cake can be easy as pie!

RUB the inside cake pan edges with margarine. Cut wax paper liners to pan size and place in bottom of pans.

PREHEAT your oven to the proper baking temperature 15 minutes (that's about the same as cake-mixing time).

FILL pans half full of batter. Place in oven and bake for the time and temperature recommended.

NO OVEN PEEKING! During the last 5 minutes of baking, check for doneness by placing a toothpick in the center of cake. When it comes out clean and layers pull away from pan edges, layers are fully baked.

COOL cakes in pans on cake rack 10 minutes. Run a knife edge around layers. Tap pan bottoms lightly. Place one cake rack on top, another on the bottom of each pan. Flip layer out and turn flat side of cake to bottom rack for cooling at least 30 minutes before frosting.

FREEZE uniced cake layers by wrapping each cooled layer in foil. Defrost about one hour before icing on busy days.

Frosting facts

PREPARE CAKE ICING according to recipe. Be sure to avoid any of those "Measuring Mistakes" on page 116.

PICTURE PERFECT cakes when you place bottom layer topside down on cake platter. Cover with frosting, then top with second layer bottomside down. Frost *sides* of cake with up-and-down strokes for a higher look.

TOP cake with remaining frosting. Smooth over cake, then swirl the top with either wide side-to-side spatula strokes or swirl from center of cake to the edges.

GARNISH with chopped nuts, candied fruits, or place leaves or flowers around edges for a special occasion.

Cooking secrets your mother may not have told you

TOUGH MUFFINS? Perhaps you baked them at too high a temperature or overmixed them. Read that recipe. It usually says "Mix until the liquid and dry ingredients are just blended."

RUBBERY EGGS? Take eggs from the refrigerator about 15 minutes before using them for breakfast or when hard-cooking them for deviled eggs. Then the word is "Cook them low and slow." For hard-cooked eggs, cover eggs with cool tap water, cover and bring water to boil. Turn off heat and allow the eggs to stand in hot water 20 minutes. Run cool water over the eggs before removing shells.

CASSEROLES, CAKES OR PIES DON'T BAKE PROPERLY? Perhaps it's *your oven*, not the recipe. Ask your local utility company to send a representative who can check the accuracy of your oven. It may need a bit of adjusting.

SOUPY SALADS? The unflavored gelatine may not have been properly dissolved. Place the envelope of unflavored gelatine in custard cup. Add proper amount of water. To dissolve the gelatine, place in pan of water over low heat for 5 to 10 minutes. Then add to other ingredients.

WHEN YOUR RECIPE

CALLS FOR	YOU'LL NEED ABOUT
2 *cups cooked noodles*	2 *cups uncooked noodles*
2 *cups cooked macaroni*	1 *cup uncooked macaroni*
4 *cups cooked spaghetti*	8 *ounces uncooked spaghetti*
4 *cups cooked rice*	1 *cup regular rice* or 4 *cups quick-cooking rice*
1 *cup grated process or American cheese*	4 *ounces cheese*

Kitchen savvy

WHY the net weight of a can is different from the measurements usually given on the label.

WHY there are different package and can sizes of the same product on the market.

WHY there are different pan sizes, casserole sizes and oven temperatures in recipes.

You've heard the common comment, "A pound's a pound the world around." That's just as out of date as the old legend that Christopher Columbus was told he'd fall off the edge of the earth as he left to explore the New World.

True, a *pound* of feathers weighs the same as a *pound* of gold, but gold takes less space. Feather space depends on whether they're down-type, feather flowers or pheasant feathers. Take Cookbook Sauces as an example. Each can contains about 1⅔ liquid measuring cups of sauce, but the net weight of the ingredients in Sweet 'n Sour Sauce is an ounce more than the others because of different sauce ingredients.

Why are there so many different package, can and jar sizes on the market? For *you*, of course! You may slip the 3-ounce jar of Coffee-mate in husband's briefcase for his office coffee breaks. Women select 6 or 11-ounce jars, depending on the family coffee-drinking habits. The 16-ounce jar is handy for camping or long vacation trips away from the local supermarket.

There are different-sized cans of products for different uses, too. If you are preparing spaghetti sauce for the crowd, the larger tomato paste or puree can is the one for you! The can sizes used by Carnation Company are listed below. Why not type up this list, then tape it inside a kitchen cupboard for use when preparing meals or making out your shopping list?

Carnation Evaporated Milk	Approximate Measurement	Net Weight
large can	1⅔ cups	14½ ounces
small can	⅔ cup	6 ounces

CONTADINA PRODUCTS

Tomato Paste	1¼ cups	12-ounce can
Tomato Paste	⅔ cup	6-ounce can
Tomato Sauce	1 cup	8-ounce can
Tomato Sauce	1⅔ cups	15-ounce can
Tomato Puree	1⅔ cups	15-ounce can
Tomato Puree	3½ cups	1-pound 12-ounce can
Tomato Puree	1¼ cups	10½-ounce can
Italian Style Tomatoes	1⅔ cups	14½-ounce can
Italian Style Tomatoes	3½ cups	1-pound 12-ounce can
Round Peeled Tomatoes	1⅔ cups	14½-ounce can
Round Peeled Tomatoes	3½ cups	1-pound 12-ounce can
Stewed Tomatoes	1⅔ cups	14½-ounce can
Stewed Tomatoes	1 cup	8-ounce can

Now it isn't possible to put every can size of every product in today's supermarket in just one cookbook. If that were done, there would be all kinds of food information and no "easy cooking" recipes in this Good-and-Easy Cookbook. For more can size information, drop a postcard to the National Canners Association, Home Economics Department, 1133 20th Street N.W., Washington, D.C. 20036. And do remember to use your zip code for faster service!

You'll frequently find that products give a net weight and more descriptive information, feminine style. Look in the supermarket and you'll find Carnation Instant Milk has a description of how many quarts of liquid nonfat milk the package will make. There are 3, 8, 14 and 20-quart packages (and would you believe a 50-quart package?) as well as 5 and 10-quart portion control envelopes!

WHY are there so many different pan and casserole sizes as well as baking temperatures given in recipes? Cooking insurance! There was a time when an equipment manufacturer, food company or food writer used different terms to describe an oven temperature. Today, after many meetings and much correspondence, there's a common way to describe various ones.

°F.	OVEN
250 and 275	Very slow
300 and 325	Slow
350 and 375	Moderate
400 and 425	Hot
450 and 475	Very hot
500 and 525	Extremely hot

The same cooperation made it possible to standardize baking dishes and pans. Notice how frequently you describe a kitchen casserole by its use—"May I borrow your lasagne dish?" What you really mean is a 13 x 9 x 2-inch ovenproof baking dish.

SHALLOW RECTANGULAR BAKING DISHES

13 x 9 x 2 inches	3 quarts
12 x 8½ x 2 inches	2 quarts
10 x 6 x 2 inches	1½ quarts

SQUARE BAKING DISHES

8-inch square
9-inch square

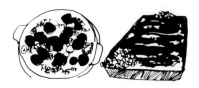

LOAF PANS

8½ x 4½ x 2¾ inches

9 x 5 x 3 inches

7⅜ x 3⅝ x 2¼ inches

1½ quarts

2 quarts

1 quart (bread pan)

CAKE PANS
8 and 9-inch round

SPRING-FORM PANS
9 and 10-inch round

PIE PLATES
8-inch, 9-inch, 10-inch, 4-inch individual, 9 and 10-inch deep-dish pie plates.

INDIVIDUAL SALAD MOLDS
½-cup individuals come in different types of design, such as heart, shamrock, star, bell and small fluted-dome ones. There are some individual molds that hold ⅔ cups, so check the size of yours!

LARGE SALAD MOLDS
There are 4-cup, 5½, 6, 6½, 7, 8, 9 and 13-cup ones in various types of design. Be sure to measure the contents before using one. (If you don't have the proper size, place remaining salad mixture in individual molds or custard cups.)

USE the proper pan or casserole mentioned in the recipe for best results! True, a 12 x 8½ x 2-inch shallow rectangular baking dish holds 2 quarts, just the same as a 9 x 5 x 3-inch loaf pan. But ovenproof baking dishes conduct heat differently from metal pans.

Today there are lots of different types of baking dishes, but some decorative casseroles aren't ovenproof. Be sure to check the hangtag or any informative material enclosed in the kitchen equipment packaging. If you aren't sure, don't use that pretty Italian casserole for macaroni and cheese!

Index of Recipes